TOUCHING HEARTS GUIDEBOOK
Harvesting "Type A" Unbelievers

by Ralph W. Neighbour, Jr.

AVAILABLE FROM:
TOUCH Outreach Ministries, Inc.
P. O. Box 19888
Houston, TX 77224, USA
Telephone: (281) 497-7901
Fax: (281) 497-0904
AND
TOUCH International South Africa
P. O. Box 1223
Newcastle 2940, SOUTH AFRICA
Telephone: (03431) 28111
Fax: (03431) 24211

ACKNOWLEDGEMENTS

· To G. P. Rockwell, who taught me at age 15 that a burdened heart is a broken heart, and that "sales pitches" for the Gospel message are a shabby substitute for authentic, Spirit-led harvesting.

· To those scores of unbelievers I have shared with, who confirmed over and over that helping someone receive Christ as Savior and Lord requires the Gospel to be "fleshed out" by believers who *show* before they *tell*.

· To R. C. Smith, for his presentation of John 3:16 and the diagram used with it.

· To you, dear reader, for your hungry heart and your desire to be used in fields "white unto harvest" all around you. As you go in pairs from your cell group to touch searching hearts, you may be certain your Lord will empower you for your tasks.

TABLE OF CONTENTS

He was my friend.
We spoke of nearly
everything
but Christ.

I denied him this.

Peter, *you* denied . . .
Yet lived to say,
"Forgive me, friend!"

I can only weep.
My friend lives
in hell forever.

INTRODUCTION
ABOUT THIS BOOK . . .

This manual equips you to bring searching unbelievers in your *oikos*—"your circle of influence"—to Christ. You will do this by partnering with another member of your cell group. Together, you will lead others to accept Christ as Lord and be nurtured in your group.

The primary task of every Christian is to bring others into the Kingdom of God. This causes each cell group to multiply as it swells with new believers. You can expect the Holy Spirit within you to empower you as you share your faith.

Touching hearts isn't *taught*—it's *caught*. This means you need to gain experience by working with someone who has *already* brought someone to Christ. Has your partner experienced the joy of bringing someone to Christ? If so, he or she can serve as your "Equipper." If this is not the case, the two of you should seek assistance from your cell leader or the cell leader intern as you reach out. You will soon know the joy of harvesting!

REVIEW OF MATERIALS . . .

PART ONE
The first part of this manual is prepared to train you and your partner in a *TOUCHING HEARTS SEMINAR* for cell group members.

PART TWO
The second part provides you with *DAILY GROWTH GUIDES*. Faithfully do these five days each week for five weeks. They will reinforce what you learned in the Seminar. As you begin to share with others, you will find this material to be very helpful. It is the result of others who have had years of experience in touching hearts. You will profit greatly from this daily devotional guide.

PART THREE
The third part is to be used during the *SHARE THE VISION* time in your cell group. Transparently share each week what God is doing in your ministry to unbelievers.

SCRIPTURE MEMORY VERSES
In addition to John 3:16, there are four other scripture memory verses you will find helpful. These verses are included in the back of this book.

YOUR OIKOS WORLD

OIKOS: MY PERSONAL COMMUNITY

Who are the people in your oikos? Write their names below. Tick the spiritual condition of each one:

	TYPE A	TYPE B	CHRISTIAN	DON'T KNOW
RELATIVES:				
1. _____	☐	☐	☐	☐
2. _____	☐	☐	☐	☐
3. _____	☐	☐	☐	☐
4. _____	☐	☐	☐	☐
5. _____	☐	☐	☐	☐
	TYPE A	TYPE B	CHRISTIAN	DON'T KNOW
FRIENDS:				
1. _____	☐	☐	☐	☐
2. _____	☐	☐	☐	☐
3. _____	☐	☐	☐	☐
4. _____	☐	☐	☐	☐
5. _____	☐	☐	☐	☐

NEIGHBORS (People who live near you):	TYPE A	TYPE B	CHRISTIAN	DON'T KNOW
1. _____	☐	☐	☐	☐
2. _____	☐	☐	☐	☐
3. _____	☐	☐	☐	☐
4. _____	☐	☐	☐	☐
5. _____	☐	☐	☐	☐

ASSOCIATES (Work or school):	TYPE A	TYPE B	CHRISTIAN	DON'T KNOW
1. _____	☐	☐	☐	☐
2. _____	☐	☐	☐	☐
3. _____	☐	☐	☐	☐
4. _____	☐	☐	☐	☐
5. _____	☐	☐	☐	☐

☺ ☺ *TALK IT OVER*

HOW MANY "TYPE A" UNBELIEVERS ARE IN THE OIKOSES OF YOU AND YOUR PARTNER?: _____

AS AN *OIKONOMOS*, YOU MUST EVALUATE THE SPIRITUAL DECISION PROCESS!

The "Type A" unbelievers you have listed are at one of these stages in their journey to Christ:

☺ ☺ *TALK IT OVER*

**WHO FITS THESE CATEGORIES?
WRITE THEIR NAMES BESIDE THE STAGES
IN THE LEFT HAND COLUMN:**

STAGE	CHARACTERISTIC
1	*Ready to pray to accept Christ; does not know how to do so. Needs help.*
2	*Has come a long way. Needs to be challenged to make the decision.*
3	*Ready to meet with you for a few sessions and learn what the Bible says about salvation.*
4	*Awareness of personal needs. Has not yet connected it to becoming a Christian.*
5	*Positive attitude toward the Gospel. Respects your faith. Has not considered following you into the Kingdom.*
6	*Appreciates your friendship. Freely shares about matters of common interest.*

☺ ☺ ***TALK IT OVER***

LIST ALL THE "TYPE A" PEOPLE YOU AND YOUR PARTNER KNOW:

NAMES OF "TYPE A" FRIENDS

1. _____

2. _____

3. _____

4. _____

5. _____

6. _____

7. _____

8. _____

9. _____

10. _____

11. _____

REPORT OF OUR FINDINGS
(Hold up one finger for each person in your oikos for each category)

1. Total persons taking this course: _____

2. Total "Type A" Unbelievers: _____

3. Total "Type B" Unbelievers: _____

4. Total Christians: _____

5. Total Spiritual Condition Unknown: _____

Conclusion: The persons taking this course are in contact with this total number of "Type A" Unbelievers: _____

REVIEW OF VIDEO PRESENTATION

1. YOUR OIKOS WORLD

OIKOS is a New Testament word which describes your network of relationships. Most of us have about 8-12 people we relate to on a weekly basis.

Spiritually, unbelievers in our *OIKOS* will fall into the five categories shown in this pyramid:

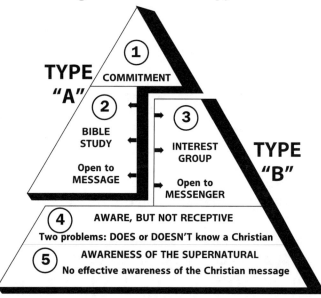

The reason this information is shown as a pyramid is to remind you that in the world there are far more people at the lower levels than at the higher ones. Every unbeliever we meet can be classified in one of the sections of this pyramid.

"TYPE A" UNBELIEVERS:
THE "LIKE US" PEOPLE, EASILY REACHED

1. They are willing to attend a celebration or a special cell group meeting.
2. They already believe in God, accept the Bible, understand that Jesus is the Son of God, and have some awareness of scripture facts (like Christ's death on the cross).
3. They may already have a church membership somewhere, but are inactive—perhaps have been so for years.
4. They are searching for something.
5. They may not have all the "pieces of the puzzle" in place as far as Christian knowledge is concerned.
6. Bible Study or explaining the plan of Salvation are appropriate activities to do with them.

"TYPE B" UNBELIEVERS: UNREACHED PEOPLE, NEEDING CULTIVATION

1. They have no interest in the Christian faith.
2. They may not believe in God, do not accept the Bible, do not understand Jesus is the Son of God, and have little awareness of scripture.
3. They have no church membership.
4. They are not searching for the Lord's purpose for their lives, and have no intention of visiting church activities.
5. They have very few of the "pieces of the puzzle" in place as far as Christian knowledge is concerned.
6. Bible Study or discussing the plan of Salvation aren't appropriate activities to do with them at the start. There must first be a time of developing relationships—exposing them to the reality of the living Christ in our own lives.

You and your partner will spend the next few weeks learning how to reach "Type A" unbelievers. Following that, you will be shown how to sponsor "Interest Groups" to reach "Type B" unbelievers.

2. THE "MAN OF PEACE"
(Luke 10:1-7)

1. Step One: "Go!"
2. Step Two: Meet *everyone* in the *oikos*.
3. Step Three: Offer your peace (Christ) to all.
4. Step Four: Once the "man of peace" has accepted Christ, *stay there*. This will begin a chain reaction in the *oikos*.

☺ ☺ **TALK IT OVER**

At which of the PYRAMID LEVELS would it be possible to:

_____ **Study the Bible together?**

_____ **Share your conversion testimony?**

_____ **Go on a biking or hiking trip?**

_____ **Invite a friend to attend a Celebration?**

_____ **Invite a friend to receive Christ?**

_____ **Invest time developing a friendship?**

_____ **Meet family (*oikos*) members?**

LUKE 10:1-9 TELLS US HOW TO MEET "TYPE A" PEOPLE NOT IN OUR *OIKOS*:

*Luke 10:1 After this the Lord appointed seventy-two others and sent them **two by two** ahead of him to every town and place where he was about to go. 2 He told them, "The harvest is plentiful, but the workers are few. Ask the Lord of the harvest, therefore, to **send out** workers into his harvest field. 3 Go! I am sending you out **like lambs among wolves**. 4 Do not take a purse or bag or sandals; and **do not greet anyone on the road**. 5 "When you enter a **house**, [OIKOS] first say, 'Peace to this **house** [OIKOS].'*

*6 If **a man of peace** is there, your peace will rest on him; if not, it will return to you.*

*7 **Stay in that house** [OIKOS], eating and drinking whatever they give you, for the worker deserves his wages. **Do not move around** from house [OIKOS] to house [OIKOS].*

THEY WERE SENT OUT IN PAIRS

THEY WERE COMMISSIONED BY GOD

THEY DEPENDED ON THE SHEPHERD'S PROTECTION

THEIR WORK REQUIRED TOTAL CONCENTRATION

THEIR CONTACT WAS TO BE WITH *OIKOSES*

THEY WERE TO SEARCH FOR "A MAN OF PEACE"

THEY WERE TO REMAIN FOR FURTHER HARVEST

THEY WERE TO REMAIN WITH RESPONSIVE SEGMENTS

8 "When you enter a town and are welcomed, **eat what is set before you.**

| THEY WERE TO CONSTANTLY RELATE TO PEOPLE |

9 **Heal the sick** who are there and tell them,

| THEY WERE TO MANIFEST GOD'S POWER |

'The kingdom of God is near you.'"

| THEY WERE TO DECLARE THE REIGN OF GOD |

☺ ☺ *TALK IT OVER*

THINK OF AN *OIKOS* YOU KNOW ABOUT THAT HAS ALREADY HAD A CHAIN OF CONVERSIONS:

YOUR LIST	YOUR PARTNER'S LIST
NAME OF FIRST BELIEVER:_____	**NAME OF FIRST BELIEVER:**_____
NAMES OF OTHERS WHO FOLLOWED:	**NAMES OF OTHERS WHO FOLLOWED:**

WHEN YOU HAVE FINISHED, WRITE IN YOUR BOOK THE NAMES OF THOSE IN YOUR PARTNER'S LIST.

3. SHARING YOUR WITNESS

"Who or what was responsible for your coming to Christ?"

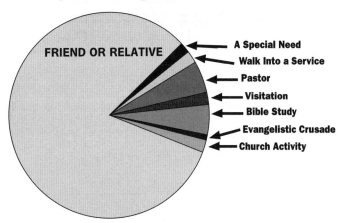

The highest percentage of believers are reached by the witness of a friend or relative!

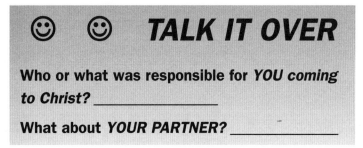

☺ ☺ **TALK IT OVER**

Who or what was responsible for *YOU coming to Christ?* _____

What about *YOUR PARTNER?* _____

DO YOU REMEMBER YOUR FIRST LOVE?

Did you have to take a *class* to learn how to express your love for that person? Cal Thomas writes, *"Some classes on evangelism may be very good, but I've never taken one. I can't remain silent about Christ. I love Him. I would have to take classes on ways **not** to talk about Him or demonstrate His love. Those who truly love Him cannot remain silent."*

Your testimony may involve two areas:
A. Events *leading up to* your conversion.
B. Situations *since* your conversion that have shown you His love and protection.

A. EVENTS LEADING UP TO YOUR CONVERSION

On the next page, there is an example of Paul's testimony, relating the events leading up to his conversion. On page 16, there is an outline for you to use in preparing a report of the events leading up to *your* conversion. If you have already completed this when you reviewed the *Journey Guide,* rewrite it again to refresh your memory.

PAUL'S TESTIMONY *(Taken from Acts 20 and 22)*

My life before becoming a Christian was like this:

I am a Jew, born in Tarsus of Cilicia, but brought up in this city. Under Gamaliel I was thoroughly trained in the law of our fathers and was just as zealous for God as any of you are today. I persecuted the followers of this Way to their death, arresting both men and women and throwing them into prison, as also the high priest and all the Council can testify. I even obtained letters from them to their brothers in Damascus, and went there to bring these people as prisoners to Jerusalem to be punished.

This is the way I realized that I needed to follow Jesus:

About noon as I came near Damascus, suddenly a bright light from heaven flashed around me. I fell to the ground and heard a voice say to me, "Saul! Saul! Why do you persecute me?" "Who are you, Lord?" I asked. "I am Jesus of Nazareth, whom you are persecuting," he replied. My companions saw the light, but they did not understand the voice of him who was speaking to me.

These are the details of how I actually accepted Christ:

"What shall I do, Lord?" I asked. "Get up," the Lord said, "and go into Damascus. There you will be told all that you have been assigned to do." My companions led me by the hand into Damascus, because the brilliance of the light had blinded me. "A man named Ananias came to see me. He was a devout observer of the law and highly respected by all the Jews living there. He stood beside me and said, 'Brother Saul, receive your sight!' And at that very moment I was able to see him."

This is what it means to me to be a Christian:

"I consider my life worth nothing to me, if only I may finish the race and complete the task the Lord Jesus has given me—the task of testifying to the gospel of God's grace."

Now, it's *your* turn! Your conversion may not have been as dramatic as Paul's. Like snowflakes, no two conversion testimonies are identical. That's what makes them special. God's call to each one of us is very personal.

As you prepare your own testimony, select one of the "Type A" persons from page 9, and visualize how you will share your story with this person.

MY TESTIMONY

My life before becoming a Christian was like this:

_____

_____

_____

_____

_____

This is the way I realized that I needed to follow Jesus:

_____

_____

_____

_____

_____

These are the details of how I actually accepted Christ:

_____

_____

_____

_____

_____

_____

_____

This is what it means to me to be a Christian:

_____

_____

_____

_____

_____

Close by asking, "Has this ever happened to you?"

TALK IT OVER

B. SITUATIONS *SINCE* YOUR CONVERSION THAT HAVE SHOWN YOU HIS LOVE AND PROTECTION.

Is Satan whispering in your ear, "You are not worthy to tell unbelievers about your Lord. Look at what a mess your life is in." Tell him to flee! He is the accuser, and you are his target.

When you became a Christian, Jesus Christ came to live in you. He is your *only* righteousness. You will never, ever have a righteousness of your own to brag about. Therefore, sharing *your* story is actually sharing *His* story—the report of what He has done in you and for you.

You have many stories you can share with "Type A" Unbelievers—occasions when you found Him sufficient for the situations you faced.

Reflect on the list below. Have you faced any of these issues? Was He sufficient for you? Then these events are a part of your story! Tick the ones that have touched your life directly or indirectly:

☐ Death of family member	☐ Divorce
☐ Marital Separation	☐ Jail term
☐ Personal Injury	☐ Serious Illness
☐ Marriage	☐ Fired from job
☐ Pregnancy	☐ Sexual problems
☐ Debts piling up	☐ Change in social activities
☐ Change in residence	☐ Auto accident
☐ Change in schools	☐ Change of employment
☐ Bad grades	☐ Trouble with boss
☐ Family conflicts	☐ Trouble with in-laws
☐ Suicidal thoughts	☐ Son/Daughter leaving home
☐ Change in sleeping habits	☐ Retirement
☐ Change in eating habits	☐ Mortgage or loan
☐ Change in finances	☐ Death of a close friend
☐ Vacation	☐ Cancer
☐ Breakup with boy/girl friend	☐ Heart Attack
☐ Guilt over past activities	☐ Stress at holiday seasons
☐ Birth of a child	☐ Abortion
☐ Stress at work/school	☐ Promotion
☐ Finishing school	☐ Rejection by family
☐ Entering military service	☐ Decision to leave home
☐ Leaving military service	☐ Change of vocation
☐ Change in number of family gatherings	☐ Change in recreation
	☐ _____
☐ Change in church activities	☐ _____
☐ Falling in love	☐ _____

Your life contains many events that parallel those in the lives of unbelievers. As you share the way Christ met your needs in those same situations, you will present a wonderful report of God's care. This may lead to an opening to pray for a situation being faced by the unbeliever.

☺ ☺ **TALK IT OVER**

SHARE WITH YOUR PARTNER ONE EXAMPLE OF HOW CHRIST MET A SPECIAL NEED IN YOUR LIFE:

_____

_____

_____

_____

_____

4. SHARING JOHN 3:16, PART 1

△ **1** COMMITMENT

As you share your testimony, the Spirit of Christ in you will let you know when the "Man of Peace" is ready to consider the message of Christ's love. *Be bold! Be brave! The Lord your God is in you!* He will use you to bring this person to accept Him.

If you have never had the experience of helping someone accept Christ, it's important for you to hear from others how *you* will feel the first time it happens. *Consider these case histories:*

CASE HISTORIES *(Take notes)*

_____

_____

_____

_____

_____

_____

_____

18

INSTRUCTIONS: WRITE OVER THE DIAGRAM AS IT IS EXPLAINED TO YOU.

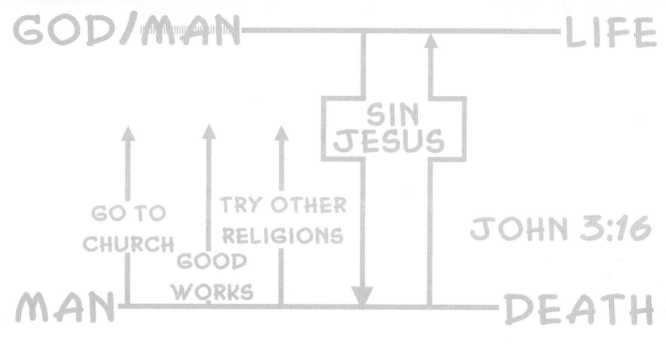

19

INSTRUCTIONS: WRITE OVER THE DIAGRAM AS IT IS EXPLAINED TO YOU.

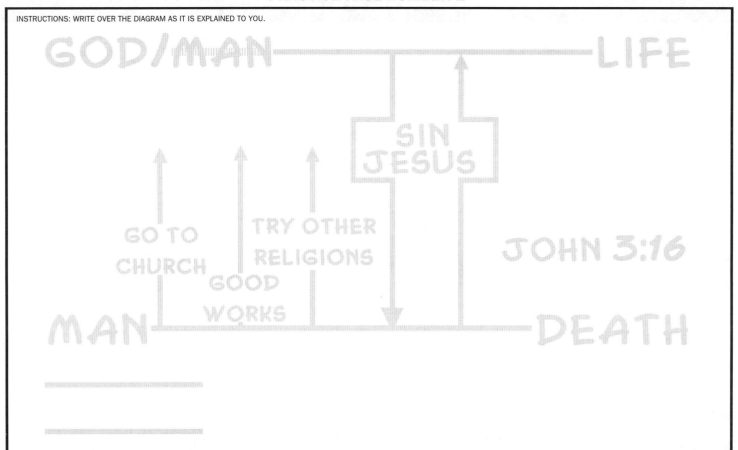

PRACTICE PAGE NUMBER 3

PRACTICE PAGE NUMBER 4

REVIEW OF VIDEO PRESENTATION

SHARING WITH THE "MAN OF PEACE"

Shake loose from old ideas.

When you visit a "TYPE A" unbeliever, you have come to a field ripe for harvest! Don't ever miss the opportunity to help a person pass from death to life.

Over the past 50 years many churches have been teaching a method of winning people to Christ very different from the pattern you are learning about. In that old pattern, the Christian did all the talking and the seeker did little more than listen. The entire pattern assumed that the Christian and the unbeliever were strangers to one another, with little or no relationship preceding or following their encounter.

Unbelievers were asked an opening question about their relationship to Jesus Christ. Usually the question related to life *after death,* not about how becoming a Christian would make a difference *today.* When the person did not give a satisfactory answer, a memorized presentation would be given with almost no interaction. If the person prayed to receive Christ, the witnessing Christian would move on to the next house. This form of outreach seemed appropriate in the past because most Christians failed to understand the relational nature of Christ's church. Too often, evangelism was an impersonal program of an impersonal church.

As a result, the church world is filled with gospel tracts and evangelism training courses which encourage two strangers to discuss God's plan of salvation without ever bothering to get acquainted with one another.

We must realize that the church is not an impersonal institution. It is Christ's body, His family, reaching out to the world. Effective outreach is done through caring relationships that make Jesus real to unbelievers through loving friendships.

You are not encouraged to become a "salesman" for the gospel, simply transmitting data to someone who "buys" your product. Instead, we must realize that the true gospel is always a *relational* gospel. (That's why the Father sent His son to the earth.) Our task is not to get others to agree that four or five thoughts are correct, pray a prayer, and then go to heaven at death.

No! Our task is to bring an unbeliever into a twofold relationship. The first relationship is with the indwelling Christ; the second is with Christ's body—a cell group. *Being a Christian is more than preparation for eternity: it's a better way to live right now.* The Christian world suffers today from millions of unattached Christians who are like dismembered parts of a human body that cannot function because they are not alive in a relationship with the other "body parts." Their "salvation" is not received until they die. That's not what Christ intended!

We are saved for all eternity as we go to the cross and exchange our sinful life for Christ's atoning life.

Immediately following that, we are to enter into a continuing salvation in which we are set free from the bondage of sin in this present life. This requires a double relationship to be established at Calvary: one with Christ, and one with the other members of His body.

LET'S READ 1 CORINTHIANS 14:24-25. In this passage, we see that in the early church a relationship between believers and unbelievers was first established:

> *. . . if . . . an unbeliever . . . enters, he is convicted by all, he is called to account by all; the secrets of his heart are disclosed; and so he will fall on his face and worship God, declaring that God is certainly among you.*

The presence of Christ was so powerful that unbelievers developed a deep desire to become a part of the Christian community. 1 Corinthians 7:14 indicates that these relationships "sanctified," or "made holy," the unsaved husband or wife. The presence of the Holy Spirit in the lives of the cell group members brought them to call on the Lord.

24

TALK IT OVER

What are the characteristics of one who is called a "Man of Peace" in Luke 10:6?

(Tick the answers you feel are true.)

☐ A bored expression when Christ is mentioned.

☐ A desire to share personal problems.

☐ A willingness to listen as you share.

☐ Openness to doing things with you.

☐ Being so busy that there is no time for you.

☐ A keen interest in what the Bible teaches.

☐ Willing to attend a get-together sponsored by your cell group.

☐ Deeply moved by your cell group's prayer life.

☐ Cynical about whether God exists.

☐ Preoccupied with personal ambitions.

☐ Heavily influenced by anti-Christian family.

Which of these comments could you use to "probe" for the responsiveness of an unbeliever? (Tick your choices.)

☐ "Have you given much thought recently to spiritual matters?"

☐ "Let's talk about Jesus for a moment. Would you share with me what you know about Him, and what you would like to know about Him?"

☐ Both of the above.

☐ Neither of the above.

HERE ARE TIMES WHEN IT'S APPROPRIATE TO SHARE HOW TO BECOME A CHRISTIAN...

· When the Holy Spirit has come to join you, and the person has a desire to talk about Jesus and His death on the cross for us.
· When your relationship has bonded you together as true friends.
· When you realize that, in spite of comments about a previous experience, the person really doesn't understand what it means to be a true Christian and needs Christ in his/her life.

SUMMARY

1. BEFORE YOU SHARE CHRIST, BUILD A TRUST RELATIONSHIP. Your sharing should be built on a mutual trust and respect for one another.

2. PROBE FOR RESPONSIVENESS
   - "Have you given much thought recently to spiritual matters?"
   - "Let's talk about Jesus for a moment. Would you share with me what you know about Him, and what you would like to know about Him?"
   - "Have you been wondering why we exist?"

3. INTRODUCTORY REMARKS
   - "Like you, I have also pondered the meaning of life. Then I ran across a little diagram that helped me put answers together that have changed my existence. Would it be okay with you if I draw it for us?"
   - *Agree to the amount of time you are going to take before you begin . . .*
   - "Could I take 15 minutes of your time?"

REVIEW OF VIDEO PRESENTATION

A. HOW TO DRAW THE NET

1. Ask, "Have you ever come to the crossroad, and made a deliberate decision to follow Jesus' pathway to God?" "Would you like to make this decision now?"
2. Three Responses:
   A. "YES."
   1. Ask three questions:
      a. Do you know that you are a sinner?
      b. Do you know your sin separates you from God?
      c. Do you want to turn from your sin? That is, do you desire to surrender the control of your life to Jesus Christ?
   2. Say, "I can't take you beyond this point. Making your decision to follow Christ is very personal. With your permission, I'm going to pray and then let you meet the Lord and personally ask Him to become your Saviour and your King."
   3. Pray, "Lord Jesus, I thank you for the privilege of sharing your love with ____. Now, let me get out of the way and let him/her talk directly to you.

4. With your head bowed, say: "I have gone as far as I can with you. You must take the final step to Jesus by yourself. Let me be a listener as you go to Him. Ask Him to forgive you for your sin and taking His place as the god of your life. Ask Him to become your Saviour and Lord."

5. Listen as your friend prays. You may have to help with the words. If you have the person repeat a prayer after you, be sure it is coming from the heart and not just the lips. If you do provide the words to the prayer, finish it and then ask the person to talk directly to Jesus without your assistance and thank them for coming into his/her life.

6. Help the person to witness. Ask, "Who is the closest friend you have—the person you share with the most?" (Let this name be mentioned.) Ask, "Why don't you let me go with you to meet your friend, and I will silently pray for you as you share this decision you have made?"

7. **Very, very important!** Present the person with the booklet *Welcome To Your Changed Life!* (Carry one in your Bible at all times to be prepared for this moment.)

B. "NO."
  1. Confirm the person's choice.
    a. Say, "It seems you don't feel God's strong call to receive Christ as your Lord. Am I correct?" Let the person reply; then pray: "Lord Jesus, I know that becoming Your child does not begin with what we desire, but rather with your strong call to follow you. I sense my friend is not hearing your call at this time. I ask you to protect what I have shared so Satan will not steal the good seed I have planted in these past moments. Help my friend remember what I have shared, and give him/her a strong desire to become Your child."
    b. Turn to "MY PRAYER LIST" in the back of your Bible. Provide a pen and present the page to be signed.

c. Say, "I have a daily time when I pray for those I have shared with. Would you write your name for me on my prayer list?"

d. Share your appreciation for the time given to share God's love. Promise to pray that the Lord will soon become very real to your friend.

C. "I AM NOT READY."
1. Establish the meaning of the statement.
   a. Say, "I sense there is a problem you have which is keeping you from feeling free to accept Christ." Let the problem be shared. Understand and discuss it. Do not pressure the person to make a decision at this time unless the Holy Spirit places a strong sense of urgency in your heart.
   b. Explain there is a prayer that is called the "Seeker's Prayer." Turn in your Bible to Hebrews 11:6 and let the person read it aloud: *"And without faith it is impossible to please Him, for he who comes to God must believe that He exists, and that He is a rewarder of those who seek Him."*
2. Suggest the person pray: "May I suggest you tell the Lord you are truly seeking Him, and that you would like Him to show you the moment when you will be able to accept Him as your Saviour and Lord?"
3. Ask the person to sign your Prayer List in the back of your Bible. Promise to pray consistently for the time when the person will be ready. Then, close with a prayer for God to bless this person.

D. IN ALL CASES, present the person with the booklet *Welcome To Your Changed Life.* It will be a way of leaving on deposit what you have said to the person. Even if the person has not accepted Christ, it will bear fruit to do this!

TALK IT OVER

(Take 6 minutes . . .)

Share with each other:

1. Any previous experiences in sharing Christ with an unbeliever you have had, and what was said when the person was invited to receive Christ.

2. If either of you received Christ through another person praying with you, try to recall how the invitation to pray was presented to you. *(If you were both converted through an invitation given in a meeting, skip this.)*

3. If you have time, use pages 26-28 to rehearse the responses you will use if a person says, "Yes," "No," or "I'm not ready."

 # REVIEW OF VIDEO PRESENTATION

B. HOW TO HANDLE EXCUSES

1. *Don't use the "Ping Pong Method!"*
   A. Trading answers about excuses is futile—even if you quote scripture to prove your point. Quoting the Bible is very important if the person is seeking answers, but it does little good if you ignore the true motives behind the delaying tactics of an unbeliever.
   B. If a person is avoiding the need to accept Christ, realize the Holy Spirit is being resisted. Arguing will be counterproductive.
2. *Don't use the "Debate Method!"*
   A. You cannot win a person to Christ by debating issues. Even if you win the debate, you'll lose the person!
   B. It is better to probe for the reasons behind the argument.
3. *Don't Argue!*
   A. Refrain from doing so, no matter what is said to you.
   B. There is only one right way to handle excuses: *probe for the underlying problem.* Seek to understand what is beneath the surface.

REVIEW OF VIDEO PRESENTATION

C. FIVE PROBE PRINCIPLES

1. *Deliberate—don't debate.*
   Ask a question instead of answering the objection.

2. *Be tender—not traumatic.*
   An argumentative spirit will never draw a person to Jesus. Have a gentle spirit.

3. *Converse—don't confront.*
   John 4:1-26 reveals how Jesus handled excuses with the woman at the well. Follow His example.

4. *Respect—don't reject.*
   If you make your friend feel inferior because he/she is not a Christian, you will do much harm.

5. *Love! Love! Love!*
   John 3:16 begins with, "God so LOVED the world . . ." This is the way to win others: *Love!*

  TALK IT OVER

(Take 10 minutes . . .)

Taking turns, role play the different responses you may expect to receive when completing the John 3:16 presentation: "No; "Yes," "I'm not ready." In each case, begin by saying:

"I have gone as far as I can with you. You must take the final step to Jesus by yourself. Let me be a listener as you go to Him. Pray out loud so I can hear you. Ask Him to forgive your sin and become your Savior. Tell Him you are ready for Him to become your Lord."

Your ministry should be appropriate to the response given by your partner. (Be sure you have prepared the page in the back of your Bible before beginning this activity.)

REVIEW OF VIDEO PRESENTATION

CONDUCTING AN INVESTIGATIVE BIBLE STUDY

1. If the person says, "I don't understand enough yet to make a decision," respond by saying, "I understand. I sense you feel this important decision deserves more attention on your part before you can make a commitment. I have learned to share a brief Bible study called *The Handbook for Successful Living* that has been specifically prepared for people who want to know more. Would you like to go through it with me? It has 13 parts, and we can go through them at your own pace. I would count it an honor to spend the time with you to talk about this more. Are you interested?"

2. If your friend is open to this, make an appointment to meet and review the lessons together. Do not spend longer than one hour together; shorter periods may be required.

3. Bring two copies of the *Handbook* with you to the first meeting. If your friend does not have a Bible, it would be a great idea to secure one and present it as a gift.

4. Select a secluded environment where you may be sure to remain undisturbed. If there is a telephone in the room, ask that it be taken off the hook.

5. Share one to one. The only time to violate this rule is perhaps with a husband and wife. There will be much more transparency if the two of you share this series by yourselves.

6. Review the *Practice Session* page. Explain the importance of actually writing in the answers in your booklets to gain greater understanding of the truths being discussed.

7. Be sure you, yourself, review each Study Guide in advance of the meeting.

8. Have your friend look up and *read aloud* all the verses as you share together.

9. Do not ignore the illustrations. Every one of them appear for a reason. While the Bible study shares the *information,* notice that every cartoon deals with attitudes or personal problems. Ask, "What does this cartoon say to you?" Or, "Do you identify with the thoughts expressed in this illustration?" These may provide you with special insights into needs.

10. Above all, *pray and pray and pray!* God will answer your prayers as the walls of resistance are broken down by the work of the Holy Spirit in the days you are meeting together.

11. Intercessory and warfare prayer for this person should be included in each cell group meeting during *Share the Vision* times. Pray against the strongholds that Satan has placed in this life to blind the mind, deafen the ears, and cause the eyes not to see the Kingdom.

12. Those who have preceded you in conducting investigative Bible studies have discovered there is no pattern to the time the person may wish to receive Christ. Be ready! Do not think you must complete the study before the person will be ready to accept Him.

13. Note there is a John 3:16 diagram in the booklet, which will be a natural time for you to review again the presentation. You might ask, "Do you remember what we said about this word/line/arrow in the diagram when we looked at it earlier?"

MAY GOD ANOINT YOU FOR YOUR MINISTRY!

WHERE DO YOU GO FROM HERE?

1. **Go back to your cell group.** Your Cell Leader will ask you to share the John 3:16 diagram with the cell during *Share The Vision* time.
2. **Go with your Partner to contact each "Type A" unbeliever you have listed during this training.** Seek to share John 3:16 with at least four people during the next two weeks. Not only will this complete your training with real experiences, but you will also reinforce all you have learned.
3. **Pray daily for those you are to visit.**
4. *Expect* **the Holy Spirit will have preceded you!**
5. **Turn in each of the two reports provided you in this training to your Cell Leader.** This will become your team's "Accountability Report" to the cell group.
6. **Ask other cell members for names of "Type A" unbelievers they know.** Seek to be introduced to them through some social occasion arranged by a cell member in his/her *oikos*.
7. **Always keep a copy of** *Welcome To Your Changed Life* **in your Bible.** Be prepared for an unexpected moment of harvest!
8. **Systematically complete the Daily Growth Guides** which follow in this book.
9. **Review** *A Handbook for Successful Living* **until you are familiar with it.**

FOLLOW THIS COUNTDOWN CALENDAR

The material in the *Touching Hearts Guidebook* provides you with five weeks of review, covering everything you have learned in the *Touching Hearts Seminar*. Since this period in your Christian life is designed to prepare you for a lifetime of ministry, it is important that you do not shirk the study of the materials and the ministry which is to follow your training. Follow these suggestions:

1. Select a specific time and place to review the Daily Growth Guides in this book. Try to do one unit each week. It is recommended that you create a routine for this study. Complete the Guides on your lunch break, your first activity after breakfast, etc. If you decide now when you will do this, doing it will not be lost in the old habits of your life.

2. You and your partner should decide now which one of you will become the "Equipper" to the other during the next five weeks. If one of you has had more experience in sharing with the lost, this will be the obvious choice. If not, one of you can volunteer to assume this role. It's a bit like the Sponsor-Sponsee relationship, but you are now "Partners." One of you should represent your team when reporting weekly to your cell leader.

3. Select the time you and your partner will meet privately together for a few minutes each week to discuss the materials. You have already been doing this for many weeks, and probably the best thing would be to continue that pattern. Or, the best time might be 15 minutes before the cell group meeting begins. You will do this for the next several weeks. To prepare yourselves for these accountability times, write down your thoughts as you complete each unit.

4. With your partner, schedule a specific time each week for the next several weeks to make contact with "Type A" unbelievers. Their availability will decide when you make these contacts.

5. A Report Form is provided in this booklet (page 94). Make five copies of this form. Your cell leader will ask you for them over the next five weeks and will discuss with you the progress you are making.

6. You will also be asked to tell the cell group about those you are contacting during *Share The Vision* times during the next few weeks. This will provide you with many intercessors for your ministry.

7. Your cell leader will also use *Share the Vision* times during the next few weeks to rehearse the John 3:16 diagram with the entire cell. You will be asked to make a full presentation to your cell at one of these meetings. Discuss with your cell leader the date you would like to make this presentation.

8. If you and your partner do not have adequate contacts with "Type A" unbelievers to work with, ask the cell leader to discuss this matter with the rest of the group.

9. As the cell group moves toward a church-wide *Harvest Event,* you will still be in the process of cultivating unbelievers. Use this event to bring them with you. Pray that God will draw them during this special time.

10. Seek to conduct at least one investigative Bible study using the *Handbook for Successful Living* during the next few weeks. It is important that you gain experience in doing this! Entering into the ability to share in depth with seekers is a vital part of the future ministry God will give to you. God will guide you to the proper person who is open to such a study. Be sure you have reviewed the material before each session.

IMPORTANT: From now on, always have one copy of *Welcome To Your Changed Life* in your Bible. Expect God to give you a convert, and be sure to provide a copy of this booklet to every person after you share John 3:16.

Introduction to the Daily Growth Guides

This section of your material has been prepared to shape your values to effectively reach "Type A" unbelievers. Please use these pages in a special way: *do only one Daily Growth Guide at a time.* Complete each one on a week day, using about 10 minutes a day. They can be included in your "Listening Room" times.

Savor what you read. Let the thoughts soak in, like a light rain saturating the earth. *(If you cram several Guides into one sitting, they will become like a heavy rain that runs off the surface of the ground, not doing much good.)*

Each Growth Guide begins with a scripture passage to be read. You may wish to underline these verses each day to help you recall their meaning later on.

The material is written in small "steps" called "frames." Thoughts are presented to you and then you are asked to think about their application to your life. Each **testing frame** asks you for a response. Read with a pen or pencil in your hand. Write in all the answers as you go, even if it seems foolish to you to do so: you will retain 160% more by writing your answers than by just thinking about them.

If you have any doubts about the way you have answered, mark the margin as an item to discuss with your partner when you meet each week. Those of us who wrote and tested this material will be praying for you—praying that Jesus Christ will become your source of love and compassion as you reach out to unbelievers. It is also our prayer that you will harvest at least one unbeliever each year from now on.

You ask, "Since the answers are easily reasoned out, why bother to write them out?" Writing your answers is the only way you can be sure you have learned essential points. If you do not write the answers, you will give yourself the illusion that you have grasped the material. (Why cheat yourself?) By immediately responding, you will be ready to move on. If you missed the answer, review. Let's give it a try:

The reason for writing my a_____ is to be sure I know the e_____ p_____.

Good! Did you write *essential points* in the blanks? Now, let's do a "dry run" before we launch into the first Daily Growth Guide . . .

PRACTICE SECTION

Visiting "Type A" unbelievers is the first way your cell group says, "We care about you!" You never know what high drama will unfold as you make a first visit! You'll meet searching hearts who are seeking to find peace of mind.

You'll find torn hearts that are bleeding, and need to be mended. You'll find hungry hearts, starved for true community. You'll find loving hearts, ready to be involved in the servant lifestyle of your cell group.

After making a few visits, one young Christian said, "Watching television is a waste of time. This has made me realize there's high drama everywhere—and God's power is always adequate to meet the needs we face. I'm glad I learned how to touch other people's lives!"

Jesus intended for us to continually widen our circle of ministry. There's no more powerful way to do so than by constantly making contacts with new people.

Let's meditate on some scriptures which will help us realize the importance of making contacts with "Type A" unbelievers. Ask yourself if this scripture refers to you, or only to Christians who are "different" from you:

Then Jesus came to them and said, "All authority in heaven and on earth has been given to me. Therefore go and make disciples of all nations, baptizing them in the name of the Father and of the Son and of the Holy Spirit, and teaching them to obey everything I have commanded you. And surely I am with you always, to the very end of the age." (Matthew 28:18-20)

Is this verse a universal commission, or does it apply only to "special" Christians who are given a "special" calling?
(CHECK THE BOX OF YOUR CHOICE!)
☐   It's universal. Jesus commissioned every Christian.
☐   It's not universal...refers to "special" Christians.

Are you included in Jesus' commission?

☐   Yes
☐   Unsure

If you answered "unsure," consider this scripture:

But you are a chosen people, a royal priesthood, a holy nation, a people belonging to God, that you may declare the praises of Him who called you out of darkness into His wonderful light . . .
(1 Peter 2:9)

Is this verse referring to every single believer, or only a select few?

☐   It's universal. If you're a Christian, you're included.
☐   It's not universal...refers to "special" Christians.

Are YOU included among those who are to "proclaim the excellencies of Him who has called you"?

☐   Yes. There's no question about it. I'm included!

He told them, "This is what is written: The Christ will suffer and rise from the dead on the third day, and repentance and forgiveness of sins will be preached in His name to all nations, beginning at Jerusalem. You are witnesses of these things. I am going to send you what my Father has promised . . ."
(Luke 24:46-49)

This scripture passage gives us our specific assignment...to be "witnesses" of Christ suffering and rising again, and that all men can receive forgiveness if they will turn away from their present lifestyles.

Which of the statements below explain the meaning of being a "witness?"

☐ **You share something you have personally experienced.**

☐ **You share a truth you have not experienced.**

A witness is "one who bears evidence." It's sharing what you have personally experienced, or have personally observed in the lives of others who are Christians!

Next, consider this passage about the exclusiveness of the truth we are to present:

Salvation is found in no one else, for there is no other name under heaven given to men by which we must be saved. (Acts 4:12)

If you meet people who say, "I already have a religion," are they exempt from the clear teaching of this verse?

☐ **Yes**

☐ **No**

Later in your training, you will learn that this powerful truth is at the heart of your sharing with others—but you can't persuade people to abandon their present beliefs by arguing with them, or by criticizing their religion. Whenever you do so, you fail your Lord! Always, always remember: loving words attract; critical words repel.

You may have been told by someone that God goes through the human race selecting special people to become His children and that you can't expect *all* unbelievers to be received by Him, even if they have a desire to become Christians. Consider this verse:

This is good, and pleases God our Savior, who wants all men to be saved and to come to a knowledge of the truth. For there is one God and one mediator between God and men, the man Christ Jesus, who gave Himself as a ransom for all...
(I Timothy 2:3-6)

What limits does this passage put on Christ's offer of salvation through His shed blood?

☐ **It's very clear. He didn't exclude a single person.**

☐ **Unsure. I'll ask my Partner to discuss this with me.**

You have probably watched many Christians who have not seemed to be concerned about harvesting "Type A" unbelievers. Many of them may have been followers of Jesus for years without bringing others to Him. You ask, "Why?"

For many generations, God's people have been told that there is a vast difference between the "clergy" and the "laity." Only the professional Christian workers are expected to win the lost. Satan's lie has been rejected by the cell church! You, along with all other Christians, are the harvesters. Go—and make disciples. His power is in *you!*

Week 1, Day 1
This Unit: Our Mandate
Today: Going "Two by Two"

Read Acts 1:8

A TRUE STORY . . .

Sammy was a shy guy. He married Karen, also quiet and soft spoken. When they first attended a cell group, they agreed in advance they wouldn't return if they didn't feel comfortable around the other members.

They were pleased when they realized they weren't expected to act like extroverts. After a couple of gatherings, both of them discovered the Lord was using them in special ways. Karen felt a deep desire to pray for a woman in the group who was suffering from postpartum depression. In her own quiet way, she poured out her heart for her in a one-on-one prayer time.

Sammy's "breakthrough" came when he sensed the Lord had given him a special word from Psalm 62:2 for a man in the group who had lost his job. In those first weeks in their cell group, they regularly discovered Christ empowering them for ministries—in ways that were perfectly natural for them.

Their cell leader explained to them that they were learning to exercise their spiritual gifts, and praised them for the spiritual growth they were experiencing.

When the time came for them to take this course, Sammy said to Karen, "God made us to be the way we are. The same power of God's Spirit we've experienced in our cell group will flow through us when we go to visit "Type A" unbelievers. As long as we're naturally letting Christ's power flow through us as we visit, we'll be effective."

List three times when Christ's power stimulated you to minister to someone else in your cell group:

1. _____

2. _____

3. _____

Can you expect Him to do the same kinds of things when He flows through you as you visit new people in their homes?

☐　Obviously, yes!

☐　Unsure. I'll ask my Partner to discuss this with me.

THE "TWO BY TWO PATTERN"

Six months prior to His death, Jesus turned His attention to a district East of the Jordan River, called Perea. It was a neglected area, ignored by the religious leaders of his day. He described Perea as a place where sheep had no shepherd!

He planned to touch it with His love. To do so, He sent thirty-five teams to represent Him there. What they were told to do is exactly what you and your partner will be doing in the weeks ahead. Read Jesus' commission to them:

> After this the Lord appointed seventy others and sent them two by two ahead of Him to every town and place where He was about to go. He told them, "The harvest is plentiful, but the workers are few. Ask the Lord of the harvest, therefore, to send out workers into His harvest field. Go! I am sending you out like lambs among wolves. Do not take a purse or bag or sandals; and do not greet anyone on the road. When you enter a house, first say, 'Peace to this house.' If a man of peace is there, your peace will rest on him; if not, it will return to you."
> (Luke 10:1-6)

WHY DO YOU THINK JESUS SENT THEM IN PAIRS?

1. Their relationship to each other as Christians would be unique. It alone would be a powerful witness to those they met in Perea.
2. They would use their spiritual gifts to build up each other. Together, they would manifest God's power flowing through them as they prayed for the sick, the hurting, and the broken hearted.
3. They would be able to share a common prayer life as they offered their peace to those they met—some who would respond, and some who would ridicule.

WHY DO YOU THINK JESUS TOLD THEM THEY WERE TOTALLY DEFENSELESS?

- They had to remember He was the Shepherd, their only protection against those who would attack them.

WHY DO YOU THINK HE TOLD THEM TO CARRY NO PURSE, BAG, OR SHOES?

- They were not going to cure social problems with welfare. The power of Christ would be given to them, and with it they would manifest the ability of God to change impossible situations.

A TRUE STORY . . .

Samuel Raj is from South India, an area filled with Hindu villages where the Gospel has never been shared. When he enters a town for the first time, he visits each home. Soon, he finds a serious problem—a very ill person, or perhaps an individual suffering from demonic oppression. He fasts and prays until the person is touched by the mighty power of Christ and made whole. The astonished villagers then gather around him, asking to know more about his God. Samuel then teaches from the Bible until they understand what it means to become Christians. He remains until a new work is established, and then moves on to do the same thing in the next village.

PRAY: "Lord, rise up within my spirit with Your Spirit! Let my heart be broken with the things that break *your* heart."

WEEK 1, DAY 2
THIS UNIT: OUR MANDATE
TODAY: FINDING "THE MAN OF PEACE"

Read Luke 10:1-9

Why do you think Jesus told those He sent out two by two to enter each home, meet each person, and search for a "man of peace?" *(Check all statements you feel partially answer this question.)*

☐ The term "man of peace" means literally, "a man who is searching for peace."
☐ The first person visited may not be responsive, but may be the opening to meet a truly responsive person within the household *(oikos).*
☐ Both of the above are correct.
☐ Neither of the above are correct.

SEARCH FOR THE "MAN OF PEACE!"

You and your Partner should not concentrate only on the "Type A" person you will visit. Seek to know each person in the context of their *oikos.* Spheres of influence exist in every one of our lives. We need to consider *every* person we meet as one who may be seeking for the Lord's peace.

There are many types of people you will meet as you visit in *oikoses.* Who do you now know who fits one of these types?

☐ Unbelievers, searching for God and for meaning in life.
☐ Unbelievers, brought to a worship service by a friend.
☐ Curious unbelievers, responding to bits of information about your walk with Christ.
☐ Christians, looking for a way to follow the Master, disillusioned with traditional church life, inactive in a church for a long time.
☐ Christians in a deep crisis with no caregivers.
☐ Christians, inactive and unmotivated, possibly filled with guilt or strongholds, feeling inadequate.

This list is just a start. There are many more possibilities. Can you add two more to the list?

_____

_____

THESE ARE THE GUIDELINES FOR MAKING YOUR FIRST VISIT :

1. Seek to meet *everyone* in the house, not just the person you have come to visit. This includes children! The Lord has something in mind by sending you to make this visit. Pray earnestly you will be able to be His ambassador to *all* you meet.

2. Be a learner! What are the interests of these family members? Are there trophies on the mantle, certificates or guns on the wall? Can you discern their value systems?

Are there antiques, or is their furniture very simple? Is the house "lived in," or flawlessly clean?

3. Get acquainted with one another by sharing answers together to the "Quaker Questions:"
   • Where did we live between the ages of 7 and 12, and how many brothers and sisters were there in our families?
   • What kind of transportation did our families use back then?
   • Who was the person we felt closest to during those years?
   • When did God become more than a word to us? (Give your own testimony at this time. It will be natural to do so!)

4. Seek to establish a bond of love and respect for one another. At the same time, determine the special needs or interests of the people you are sharing with.

5. Find a mutual area of interest, or a need in your life or theirs, which would make it a natural thing to get together for a longer visit in the near future. Make an appointment to do so if possible.

6. Say, "May I tell you a little bit about my spiritual journey?" In no more than three or four minutes, tell a bit about your own spiritual growth and what the Lord has meant to you. Then say, "We're all on a spiritual journey. Would you like to share a little bit about yours with us?"

7. If the person is responsive, ask for permission to share the John 3:16 diagram.

8. If you have not yet established a strong relationship with this person and think it would be premature to offer to share the John 3:16 diagram, decide how to invite this person or family to an activity you might do with them soon.

9. What does the Spirit say to you about this person or family? Is there receptivity when you bring up spiritual things, or do you sense a coldness, a lethargy, in their responses? If someone seems to be thirsty for spiritual growth, you will sense this. Focus on sharing deeper with this person. If not, you will hear excuses about why further contacts are not possible. If you get "pushy," a gap of embarrassment will be created by your pressing them to do something they do not desire.

10. Some who are visited for the first time will be unbelievers who think they are Christians, even though they have never made a personal commitment to Christ. Your first visit to such persons will not be your last visit. Keep the relationship open! Continue to cultivate your friendship with them. Your primary task is to bring to them the life of the Lord Jesus. Don't leave them with the impression that you are nothing more than a "cell group salesperson!"

11. Always, always close in prayer. Intercede for all problems which have been shared. Pray for God to bless this person or home with His presence. If there is a special area of need, pray for God's power to be manifested in meeting that need. Then, after you have left the home, jot down a list of needs you discerned. Begin to pray for this home daily, keeping in touch by telephone to see how the person or family are getting along.

Pray: "Lord, speak to me as I listen to those I meet. Mingle your voice with theirs, and give me your words to speak."

Week 1, Day 3
This Unit: Our Mandate
Today: The Power of Intercession

Read Ephesians 2:1-3; Matthew 21:21-22

"Type A" unbelievers need your intercessory prayers for their salvation. Ephesians 2:1-3 reminds us that Satan has caused them to be blind and deaf to the presence of the Lord. They have. . .

. . . followed the ways of this world and of the ruler of the kingdom of the air, the spirit who is now at work in those who are disobedient.

They are spiritually handicapped. They live in darkness. They have no awareness of God's great desire to bring them new life. They are like blind men walking toward a cliff, unaware of the destruction before them.

PRAYER OPENS THE CLOSED HEART

Bringing unbelievers to Christ does not begin with speaking words to them. Your ministry begins with broken-hearted words to God about the strongholds implanted in their lives. The unbeliever cannot *hear or see* spiritual truths.

Matthew 21:21-22 brings a new dimension to their condition:

If you believe, you will receive whatever you ask for in prayer.

Praying for the lost is a vital part of bringing them to faith. As you visit with "Type A" unbelievers, become aware of the ways they are blinded to God's presence.

How many of these strongholds exist in the life of a "Type A" unbeliever on your list?

☐ Obsessed with work.

☐ Preoccupied with sexual films and books.

☐ Addicted to drugs, sports, or pleasure activities.

☐ Filled with mistrust because of past experiences.

☐ Inner anger because of being wronged by another.

☐ Deep insecurity about becoming poor.

☐ Feelings of worthlessness; obesity; withdrawn.

☐ Hyperactive, never stopping to think deeply.

☐ _____.

☐ _____.

Create a prayer list describing the spiritual needs in the life of each unbeliever you desire to bring to Jesus. Conduct spiritual warfare against those strongholds, crying out to God to release the person from their bondage. You will be delighted when you see them respond to God's voice!

A TRUE STORY . . .

Chester and his wife joined Ruth and me to launch a new cell group. His wife had a brother who had lost his driver's license for drunk driving. He was living with a Mexican woman with two daughters, also an alcoholic. The two of them fought constantly. She warned him that if he ever tried to leave her, she would kill him.

Finally, this man moved out of the apartment, disgusted with the constant fighting. She got very drunk and came to the auto parts store where he worked. Taking a car jack, she began smashing out the windows of the store, knocked over all the racks of merchandise, and attacked him. She tore open his shirt and clawed his chest with her fingernails, the damage requiring 73 stitches. It took five policemen to handcuff her and take her to jail. The man moved back in with her, frightened about what else she might do to him.

Chester invited this man to attend our cell group. He was a "Type A" unbeliever! I made an appointment to meet him for lunch the next day. Using the back side of a paper place mat, I shared the John 3:16 diagram with him. He immediately accepted Christ as his Lord.

It was then he told me about the woman he lived with, asking for counsel. I asked him to list the spiritual strongholds in her life. They included: fear, insecurity, alcohol abuse, violent temper and past beatings by her husband in Mexico. We prayed together for their power over her to be broken. I then suggested he invite her to come to our cell group.

My friend said, "I don't think she would *ever* consider that!" I responded, "You are not factoring in the prayer warfare for her that has started. You may be surprised."

That night, he told her of his decision to follow Christ and asked her to visit the cell group with him. To his shock, she immediately agreed to do so.

Her first visit with us was very meaningful. We focused all our attention on her, using the Quaker Questions. Before the evening was over, she felt free to tell us of the horrible life she had lived in Monterrey with a violent husband, her flight to the United States with her daughters, and her inner fears. We prayed that God would give her a new awareness of His love.

The next day, upon return from work my friend found his suitcases packed and waiting for him outside the door. She said, "I went down to the *Iglesia* today and became a Christian. I want you to come and see me baptized. I will be joining your cell group, but from now on we will not sleep together. I want to show my daughters how a Christian mother should live."

By faith, write below a description of what you will trust God to do in the life of one of your "Type A" friends:

_____

_____

_____

Week 1, Day 4
This Unit: Our Mandate
Today: All Things To All Men

Read 1 Corinthians 9:19-22

Our mission is not to release information to the unbeliever. Rather, our purpose is to expose the person to the Christ who lives within us. We are seeking to bring others into a *relationship* with the living Christ. This cannot be done unless, like Paul, we are willing to become "all things to all men."

Every unbeliever lives in a private universe made up of work, friends, and interests. It is necessary to enter that universe, to become a part of it. Paul wrote,

I have become all things to all men so that by all possible means I might save some.

Your relationship with "Type A" unbelievers must begin with learning about what they are interested in, and entering in to their interest.

A TRUE STORY

As a small boy, my bedroom was next to my father's office in the parsonage. He had a heavy responsibility as pastor of a large congregation, but he also had a great love for the lost. Behind our home lived Mr. Crumley, an avid ham radio operator who had no interest whatsoever in church life. His wife and son attended church every week, but he remained at home talking to the world through his ham radio station.

Dad had a great burden for this man. He began his relationship with Mr. Crumley by visiting the "ham shack" in the basement of his home. Hours were spent learning about his electronic equipment, antennas and the "lingo" used among ham operators.

Because Dad's pastoral duties demanded long hours, his relationship with this man had to be squeezed between other tasks. Finally, Crumley offered to set up a ham radio system for Dad if he would qualify himself by earning a license. This meant becoming proficient in using Morse Code—the equivalent to mastering shorthand or perhaps a foreign language!

The only time Dad had to practice was late at night, about the time I would be going to sleep in the adjacent room. The clack-tick-clack of the telegraph key disturbed me, and I went into his office to see what he was doing. Dad put his arm around me and said, "Ralph, your playmate, Jimmy, has an unsaved Daddy. I want to win him to Jesus. The only way I can get inside his life is to become a ham radio operator. When you hear me practicing in here, please pray that God will touch Mr. Crumley's heart."

Dad passed the license exam and installed equipment in the basement of our house. Soon the two men were moving back and forth between their basements. In the midst of their activity, the Christ who controlled my father's life drew this man to the Cross.

I shall never forget the night when Mr. Crumley accepted Christ in our living room! He became very active serving Christ in the following years.

REACH "TYPE A" UNBELIEVERS THROUGH RELATIONSHIPS

What will it take to develop a "heart trust" relationship with *your* "Type A" unbeliever? Do not think of your ministry as selling a "product." Instead, form a friendship that will continue for months as you become fellow Christians in your cell group.

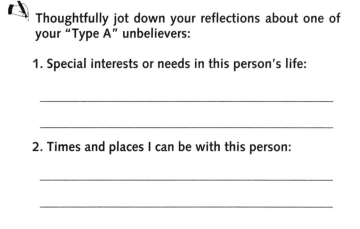 Thoughtfully jot down your reflections about one of your "Type A" unbelievers:

1. Special interests or needs in this person's life:

_____

_____

2. Times and places I can be with this person:

_____

_____

_____

> # REMINDER
>
> You and your partner should take about 15 minutes to review
> **A HANDBOOK FOR SUCCESSFUL LIVING**
> Do so each week until you feel you are familiar with the materials.
> (You'll never know when you will need it!)

45

WEEK 1, DAY 5
THIS UNIT: OUR MANDATE
TODAY: REVIEW JOHN 3:16 DIAGRAM

Read 2 Timothy 4:2

". . . be prepared in season and out of season . . ."

Which of these times would be appropriate to share the way you became a Christian with a "Type A" unbeliever? (Check all statements you feel partially answer this question.)

☐ When the Holy Spirit speaks to you to do so.

☐ When the person desires to listen to what you say.

☐ When your relationship has bonded you together.

☐ When you realize the person really doesn't understand what it means to be a true Christian.

MEDITATE ON THIS DIALOGUE

While the following dialogue is prepared to help you think through what you might say when sharing the John 3:16 diagram, it's not meant to be memorized. After you become familiar with it, you will do best using your own words in a heart-to-heart sharing time. Avoid "canned" formulas. In real life, the thoughts related to the diagram may be presented in a different sequence, or over a period of time instead of just one session. Let the Spirit lead you!

1. INTRODUCTION

"I want to thank you for the opportunity to come by and visit with you. I'd like to share a little bit about myself . . ." (Take time to build a "trust" relationship.)

2. PRESENTATION

"Could we speak about the meaning of life? I'd like to ask you what you have found it to be, and then perhaps you would let me also share." (Let the other person share views on the meaning of life.)

"Like you, I've also pondered over this. And then I ran across a little diagram that helped me put together answers that have changed my whole existence. Would it be okay with you if I draw it now? (Use a blank sheet of paper.)

"I have difficulty grasping things when there's a lot to think about. Could I take about 10-15 minutes to share this with you?" (Be sure the person has the time!)

On the top of the left side of the paper, write:

GOD   Step 1: God Created us.

"First of all, let me share a basic truth that most people will agree to: that there is a God, and He is eternal. Would you agree to that truth?" (Let the person share. Do not be in a hurry!)

"God has the right and the power to do whatever He chooses to do. I'd like to share with you a marvelous truth about God. He created man, and made us for a specific purpose, which is to have fellowship and enjoy Him forever."

GOD/MAN Step 2: God made man to have fellowship with him.

That's a marvelous thing for us to think about: God, who had the power to make us in the beginning, intended for us to live our lives here on earth in fellowship with Him. Have you ever thought about that?" (Let the person discuss this with you.)

"If God created us, and if He wanted us to live our daily lives in fellowship with Him, then we have a problem. I don't mind sharing with you that many things happened in my life to make me know I was apart from God."

"But the beautiful thing about the way He created us is that He breathed life into man, and then gave us the right to make our own choices, to freely make our own decisions."

GOD/MAN **LIFE**

STEP 3:

God desired for that relationship to be eternal. That's why He created us to live forever, so we could always be with Him.

God did not make us robots. I'm glad He didn't, because

He made us in His own image, and we can choose whatever we'd like to do with our lives.

GOD/MAN——————LIFE

STEP 4:

God desired to guide each decision made by us, so the true meaning of life would always be experienced by us.

The sad news is that man chose to do his own thing! Thus, He chose to separate himself from God. This was man's choice, not God's. That's important to realize. Our dilemma is one we have manufactured for ourselves.

GOD/MAN————LIFE

MAN

STEP 5:

God didn't make us robots. He gave us the freedom to choose whether we would agree to His guiding our lives. Mention Adam and Eve's decision to reject His control over their lives. One by one, we have all made the same choice!

Tick any of the Steps in this first review that you feel you need to concentrate on. Be sure you fully grasp what you will be sharing with "Type A" unbelievers.

☐ Step 1   ☐ Step 3   ☐ Step 5

☐ Step 2   ☐ Step 4

WEEK 2, DAY 1
THIS UNIT: OUR MESSAGE
TODAY: FREE FROM SIN'S PENALTY

Read Hebrews 9:15 and 26; Colossians 2:13-15

INTRODUCTION TO THIS WEEK'S MATERIALS

The *Year of Equipping* training you are taking is a very crucial time in your Christian life. Without apology, it is a rigorous training! Soldiers never go into battle without proper drills. A part of your being equipped is for your *understanding of salvation* to be confirmed. If you do not fully understand what our salvation involves, you could be very injurious to a "Type A" unbeliever. Bad counsel for searching unbelievers might seriously damage their Christian life.

If, at the end of this week's study, you still are unclear about what you will be taught, continue to discuss the scripture's teaching about salvation with your cell leader or your pastor. Clarifying this area is vital not only to what you share with others, but for your own growth as well.

To illustrate the danger: in 1994, the largest evangelical denomination in America reported that *65% of their reported "new conversions" were in fact people who had previously made a confession of faith and had been baptized!* These were all people who were so dissatisfied with their previous commitment to Christ that they were asking for rebaptism. They are the direct result of "Type A" unbelievers who were not fully taught there are *three* aspects to salvation, not just one. In this week's materials, we will carefully examine the scriptures about all three. We must begin with . . .

1. THE FINISHED WORK OF THE CROSS: OUR PENALTY PAID

When we come to the Cross, salvation begins when we exchange our rebellious life for the righteous life of Jesus. We give Him our life; He gives us His life! At that moment, we are forever set free from the *penalty* of sin. Consider these verses (Hebrews 9:26, Colossians 2:13-15):

But now he has appeared once for all at the end of the ages to do away with sin by the sacrifice of himself.

When you were dead in your sins and in the uncircumcision of your sinful nature, God made you alive with Christ. He forgave us all our sins, having canceled the written code, with its regulations, that was against us and that stood opposed to us; he took it away, nailing it to the cross. And having disarmed the powers and authorities, he made a public spectacle of them, triumphing over them by the cross.

Does the death of Christ on the cross set us free from the *penalty* of sin? Yes! Hebrews 9:26 says He died *"once for all!"* Is our salvation from the penalty of sin (remember, we are not referring to "sins" here) a completed action? Yes! I am not holding on to God; He is holding on to me. Jesus said:

> "My sheep listen to my voice; I know them, and they follow me. I give them eternal life, and they shall never perish; no one can snatch them out of my hand. My Father, who has given them to me, is greater than all; no one can snatch them out of my Father's hand." (John 10:27-29)

If we do not adequately understand there are *three* aspects to our salvation, we may consider the blood of the cross inadequate to guarantee our eternal salvation. Those who say, "I used to be a Christian, but I lost my salvation" speak from terrible ignorance. Hebrews 6:4-6 tells us:

> It is impossible for those who have once been enlightened, who have tasted the heavenly gift, who have shared in the Holy Spirit, who have tasted the goodness of the word of God and the powers of the coming age, if they fall away, to be brought back to repentance, because to their loss they are crucifying the Son of God all over again and subjecting him to public disgrace.

In other words, if we say the blood of the cross was not adequate to keep us if we "fall away," we must not say, "Jesus, climb back up on the cross! Let me drive these spikes through your hands and feet again. The first time you died for me was not adequate. Be crucified again so we can be saved over again!" *"No, no, no!"* says the writer of Hebrews. The transaction of Calvary is a *completed action:*

> But now he has appeared **once for all** at the end of the ages to do away with sin by the sacrifice of himself. (Hebrews 9:26b)

When we come to the cross, we receive the living presence of Jesus into our lives. Salvation is having *Christ within,* not just accepting a new belief system. Paul writes:

> I have been crucified with Christ and I no longer live, but **Christ lives in me.** The life I live in the body, I live by faith in the Son of God, who loved me and gave himself for me. (Galatians 2:20)

Our relationship with Jesus started at the cross. *He lives in me!* 1 John 4:3 teaches us:

> We know that we live in him and he in us, because he has given us of his Spirit.

When you share the John 3:16 diagram, be certain that you establish the reality of Christ *literally* coming to live within our lives as we surrender the thrones of our lives to Him. Ponder this truth all day today. The next Daily Growth Guides will explain that when we come to the Cross, we *begin* our salvation by establishing a relationship with Christ. But there's more. Salvation from the penalty of sin is only the beginning!

Week 2, Day 2
This Unit: Our Message
Today: Free From Sin's Presence

Read Hebrews 9:27, Revelation 12:10; Titus 2:11-14

Hebrews 9:27 connects the first and the third aspects of salvation. Note how the writer speaks first about the finished work of the cross that brings us salvation from the **penalty** of sin:

> Just as man is destined to die once, and after that to face judgment, so Christ was sacrificed once to take away the sins of many people . . .

This passage then goes on to speak of *another* aspect of salvation that is future—the salvation we will receive in an age to come, when we will be freed from the **presence** of sin:

> . . . and he will appear a second time, not to bear sin, but to bring salvation to those who are waiting for him.

". . . *to bring salvation.*" This refers to a final aspect of our salvation, definitely waiting for all believers. However, it cannot be received until God brings this evil age to a close.

Revelation 12:10 describes the time when the kingdoms of this world, ruled over at present by Satan, shall be destroyed. The very *presence* of sin will be removed for all eternity:

> Then I heard a loud voice in heaven say: "Now have come the **salvation** and the power and the kingdom of our God, and the authority of his Christ. For the accuser of our brothers, who accuses them before our God day and night, has been hurled down."

This aspect of future salvation is what New Testament Christians called the "blessed hope" (Titus 2:11-14):

> For the grace of God that brings salvation has appeared to all men. It teaches us to say "No" to ungodliness and worldly passions, and to live self-controlled, upright and godly lives in this present age, while we wait for the blessed hope—the glorious appearing of our great God and Savior, Jesus Christ, who gave himself for us to redeem us from all wickedness and to purify for himself a people that are his very own, eager to do what is good.

Which aspect of salvation is being referred to in the above scripture?

☐   **Salvation from the penalty of sin.**

☐   **Salvation from the the presence of sin.**

☐   **It's talking about salvation both present and future.**

Actually, the third statement is not wrong. The life we now live in Christ anticipates a future time when He will establish the eternal Kingdom of God. We will reign with Him forever. With the knowledge of what is going to happen, we wait for the end of this wretched era. We have a *future salvation,* a time when there will be no more war, when lions will lie down with lambs, and men will beat their swords into plowshares.

Do you see how important it is to reveal these thoughts to "Type A" unbelievers *before* they pray to receive Christ? Tragically, many Christians have a concept of salvation that is nothing more than this:

I took out my eternal life insurance policy with God. I prayed, 'God, be merciful to me, a sinner, and save my soul for Jesus' sake.' That's all there is to it! I am glad Jesus paid the price for it on the cross. It has cost me nothing. Now I can enjoy life and pay respects to God by attending church when it is convenient. Some day (I want to believe in all this) I will die and enjoy my heavenly home. I will tolerate the preacher telling me I have an obligation to God to tithe and to come to all the church services. But in reality, I don't feel I should get too radical about all this religious stuff.

It is a solemn thing to become a *pais,* a child/servant of Jesus Christ. The future salvation from the *presence* of sin requires that our days in this life will be inspected before we enter that Kingdom. While our salvation from the *penalty* of sin was settled at Calvary, there is to be a judgment of every believer. This is clearly taught in 1 Corinthians 3:11-15:

For no one can lay any foundation other than the one already laid, which is Jesus Christ. If any man builds on this foundation using gold, silver, costly stones, wood, hay or straw, his work will be shown for what it is, because the Day will bring it to light. It will be revealed with fire, and the fire will test the quality of each man's work. If what he has built survives, he will receive his reward. If it is burned up, he will suffer loss; he himself will be saved, but only as one escaping through the flames.

Coming to the cross begins a relationship. Christ comes to dwell within us. We are no longer our own property. We belong to Him. He has every right to guide our days. If we ignore His inner guidance, making decision after decision without regard for His will, we walk in disobedience and will never conquer the presence of sin. As a believer, you have a redemptive purpose in the work of God here on earth. Therefore, our level of obedience will be considered (see 2 Timothy 2:11-13).

Think about the coming destruction of the world and the establishment of an eternal Kingdom of God in eternity. *Do you really believe it will happen?* If you have never thought this through before, it's time you do so now. Our life in Christ *today* is preparation for *tomorrow's salvation.*

Sharing these truths with unbelievers is an important part of your discussion related to the John 3:16 presentation. How will you share it? Don't wait until you are in the discussion to answer that question! Use your idle moments today to think about how you would share the truth about *salvation future,* when we will be set free from the *presence* of sin.

Week 2, Day 3
This Unit: Our Message
Today: Free From Sin's Power

Read Philippians 2:1-16

We are going to study this scripture in depth. It explains *salvation present*. First of all, review the passage and note the number of times "you" is used. In English, the pronoun "you" is used for both singular and plural. This is not true in the Greek. *Every "you" in this passage is plural.* Not one of Paul's comments were directed to an individual! In every case, He was addressing a *group* of people—those who comprised the Basic Christian Communities (cell groups) in the body of Christ at Philippi. Salvation *present* takes place in Christ's body.

Using a pen, answer the following questions:

Which aspect of salvation is being referred to in verses 12 and 13?

☐ Salvation past
☐ Salvation future
☐ Salvation present

We know that we cannot "work out" our salvation from the *penalty* of sin, because Christ canceled that by His death. We know we cannot "work out" our salvation from the *presence* of sin, for Christ must come to establish the Kingdom of God before that will take place.

SALVATION PRESENT IS THE WORK OF CHRIST IN HIS BODY

The salvation referred to in this passage is a *present salvation,* the release from the *power* of sin. As long as we live in the flesh, a war is taking place within us. Christ dwells in us, but so does our human spirit that continues to exercise our freedom of choice. (Becoming a Christian doesn't make us robots.) When the "old man" within us chooses to disregard Christ's right to be Lord over us, we forfeit receiving deliverance from the *power* of sin.

The Greek word for *work out* in verse 12 means to "toil fully in a special place or time." We do not do this independently, but with others in Christ's body, the cell group. "Work out your *(plural!)* salvation."

In verse 13, we are told that God is also working in you *(plural!)*—but the Greek for "work" is a different word altogether, meaning *"to energize."*

Let us recognize that salvation past, present or future is not a *condition*, but is always the *activity of Christ.* This truth may be made clearer by noting Simeon's statement when the baby Jesus was placed in his arms:

> *Simeon took him in his arms and praised God, saying: . . . "my eyes have seen your **salvation,** which you have prepared in the sight of all people, a light for revelation to the Gentiles and for glory to your people Israel." (Luke 2:28, 30-31)*

The resurrected Christ has come to live within His new body, the "called-out ones," who gather in small groups where He actively saves them from the power of sin. The cell group gathers to work out its deliverance, knowing that Christ within is the source of their victory.

Working out our salvation from the power of sin is not something we can do by ourselves, on our own. Underline the scripture that best confirms this for you:

Rom. 15:14: ". . . you yourselves are . . . competent to instruct one another. "

Gal. 5:13: ". . . serve one another in love."

Eph. 4:2: "be patient, bearing with one another in love."

Eph. 4:32: "Be kind and compassionate to one another, forgiving each other . . ."

Eph. 5:21: "Submit to one another out of reverence for Christ."

Phil. 2:4 "Each of you should look not only to your own interests, but also to the interests of others."

Col. 3:13 "Bear with each other and forgive whatever grievances you may have against one another."

Col. 3:16 "Let the word of Christ dwell in you richly as you teach and admonish one another . . ."

1 Thess. 5:11: "Therefore encourage one another and build each other up, just as in fact you are doing."

Hebr. 3:13: "But encourage one another daily . . ."

Hebr. 10:24: "And let us consider how we may spur one another on toward love and good deeds . . ."

THE TRAGEDY OF UNTAUGHT CHRISTIANS

Traditional churches do not understand that the Basic Christian Community, the cell group, is the way Christ works within His body to deliver us from the power of sin. Thus, a large number of Christians see the church only as an organization with programs to be supported, attended, and joined. Believing that the daily Christian walk is therefore a *private* matter, they live in bondage, never overcoming the power of sin. They have been robbed of a vital part of their salvation!

Consider the tragedy of your presenting the gospel message to an unbeliever and *not referring to this aspect of salvation.* If we speak about coming to the cross to receive freedom from the *penalty* of sin—and the assurance that if we do, "God will let us into His heaven"—we have robbed the new believer of the way the *power* of sin will be overcome. If we say, "God has a wonderful plan for your life" and exclude the truth that this involves active participation in Christ's body, we have been deceptive. We make "church" an option that has nothing *directly* to do with our salvation from sin's power. Obviously, the *church* does not save us, but *Christ with His body* brings deliverance. We must be properly related to His work within His body for this to take place.

The first official act of the Holy Spirit when we come to the cross is to baptize us into the body of Christ (see 1 Corinthians 12:13-14). Unless we are immediately attached to a cell group body of Christ, we will not be able to "work out our salvation with fear and trembling!"

Week 2, Day 4
This Unit: Our Message
Today: Sharing The Three Aspects

Read Romans 10:8-10

THE THREE ASPECTS OF SALVATION Christ sets us free from sin as a . . .		
PENALTY	**POWER**	**PRESENCE**
By His death	By His life	By His return
PARDONED	EMPOWERED	RELEASED
A POINT in time	A PROCESS of time	A POINT in time
Happens when I am tired of my sin	Happens when I am in the Body of Christ	Happens when the Lord returns
Christ lives in me	Christ delivers me by working through His Body	Christ reigns over me
I am a *little child*	I am a *young man*	I am reigning with Christ

Digest the thoughts presented to you in this chart. As you grasp these truths, you will feel confident that you have the background for the conversations you will now have with "Type A" unbelievers.

Remember . . . your times of sharing are not "canned presentations." The John 3:16 diagram gives you an outline, a track for you to run on, but it is not intended to be presented as a lecture. For the sake of brevity in training, the John 3:16 weekend took you straight through the materials, but in life it will not always be that way. Be sure to proceed at the rate of the unbeliever's responses.

A TRUE STORY

Many years ago, a Welsh lady came to my cell group. She had a husband who worked at an air force base and spent most of his pay check getting drunk on Friday nights. Their house was set back from the road, so every time I would drive up to see him he would run out the back door and disappear until I was gone.

I prayed earnestly that the Lord would arrange a way for us to get acquainted. Whether from the Lord or not, I will not say—but this man got the worst case of the gout I had ever seen. He was confined to his chair with a pillow under his foot for several days. He couldn't escape from me!

I spent the first few hours just getting acquainted, swapping stories about our childhoods and his army service. Gradually he accepted me as a friend. We came to the moment when I could ask, "I know you don't ever think about spiritual things, and you know that is the most important thing in my life. Would you permit me to share with you what I believe?"

He put a new chew of tobacco in his cheek and said, "Go ahead." I began the John 3:16 presentation. We moved rather quickly through it until I wrote the word "DEATH." He exploded! He had convinced himself there was no after-life and that hell was nonsense. So strong were his feelings that I dropped the discussion. The next day I returned to visit him. He had cooled off, but was still pondering the issue of death and eternal separation from God. It took some time to work through that area, and I had to search my concordance in the back of my Bible for answers to some of his questions.

Finally, we completed the entire presentation and he accepted Christ as his Lord. I saw that man grow and grow in the Lord as he was delivered from alcohol abuse and became a man of prayer. Sharing patiently with him worked!

THINK ABOUT HOW YOU WILL SHARE THE THREE ASPECTS

The diagram below may assist you in preparing yourself for the ways these important facts can be woven into the presentation. Let the Holy Spirit become your teacher! Ask Him to reveal to you the best way for you to explain these important facts:

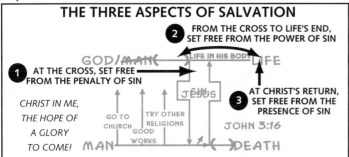

THE THREE ASPECTS OF SALVATION

2 FROM THE CROSS TO LIFE'S END, SET FREE FROM THE POWER OF SIN

GOD/MAN — LIFE IN HIS BODY — LIFE

1 AT THE CROSS, SET FREE FROM THE PENALTY OF SIN

JESUS

3 AT CHRIST'S RETURN, SET FREE FROM THE PRESENCE OF SIN

CHRIST IN ME, THE HOPE OF A GLORY TO COME!

GO TO CHURCH   TRY OTHER RELIGIONS   GOOD WORKS

JOHN 3:16

MAN — DEATH

HOW WILL YOU PRESENT THESE TRUTHS?

1. Salvation is not a way of *believing;* it is *receiving Christ.*
2. When we go to the cross, we exchange our life for the life of Christ. He comes to live within us as our Lord.
3. Christ has a special body in today's world. His body is formed by the Holy Spirit, who joins believers together to become the parts of His body.
4. When Christ comes to live in us, our first priority is to be a working member of His body, which takes the form of a Basic Christian Community, a cell group.
5. We receive freedom from the *penalty* of sin at the cross; we find freedom from the *power* of sin as we work through our spiritual strongholds with the believers in our cell group. Working out our daily salvation from the power of sin cannot be done in private. Christ performs this act of salvation through Body Life.
6. The way we mature spiritually in this life is important. One day, when He returns, we will give an account of what we did with our lives on earth. When He establishes His Kingdom, Christians will be assigned tasks based on their past obedience and performance.

Today, in your odd moments, meditate on these truths. Envision yourself explaining them to one of your "Type A" unbelievers. Think of the words you will use. Seek an anointing from the Holy Spirit to empower your words with Christ's presence.

Week 2, Day 5
This Unit: Our Message
Today: Review John 3:16 Diagram

Read Genesis 3:1-10

"You will not surely die," the serpent said to the woman. "For God knows that when you eat of it your eyes will be opened, and you will be like God, knowing good and evil."

What was the sin committed by Adam and Eve? (Check all statements you feel partially answer this question.)

☐ They desired to know as much as God knew.

☐ They did not believe God was telling the truth when He said, "when you eat of it you will surely die."

☐ They enjoyed eating a piece of fruit.

☐ They were motivated by a desire to become significant through their own choices.

☐ They were unaware of the power of Satan, who came in disguise.

☐ They acted out of ignorance and should not have been penalized by God for what they did.

UNBELIEVERS THINK "SIN" AND "SINS" ARE IDENTICAL

You may recall this diagram appears in *Welcome To Your Changed Life*. It compares a tree's roots with the fruits it bears. If the nature of the tree is *apple*, the fruit will be *apples*. Removing the apples doesn't change the tree root.

S I N

In the illustration above, put an "X" over the "S" and the "N." Then draw the letter "I" on the throne inside the heart. This is our "root problem." Think of some "sins" and write their names beside the fruit which borders the heart. Root problem = SIN; fruit of a life with "I" on the throne = SINS.

```
GOD/MAN————————————LIFE
                    SIN ✎
```

STEP 6:

Explain that "SIN" is simply living without any regard for God's will. Anything we do that rejects God's will is seen by Him as sin. Our good deeds as well as our bad deeds are unacceptable if we do them apart from His guidance and control of our lives. "All our righteous deeds are like filthy rags!"

It is unwise to move forward in your discussion until this all-important truth has been well established. If there is not a full understanding of what sin is, the cross of Christ will have no meaning. Be careful to confirm this truth!

```
GOD/MAN————————————LIFE
                    SIN

MAN                      ✎ DEATH
```

STEP 7:

The consequences of our choice are serious! God made us to live with Him forever. Our choice to refuse to be led by Him in this life is irreversible when we die. Thus, for all eternity we will continue to live apart from Him. Making this decision means we face eternal death without God!

ADD THE WORD "DEATH"

Many people falsely believe that "the Man Upstairs" will eventually agree to accept everyone into His presence. Many do not believe in a life after death. Others do not believe in an eternal separation from God for those who reject His Kingship over them.

This is another crucial point to be confirmed through discussion. Ask, "Do you believe there is a life after death?" "Do you believe those who reject God's direction while in this life are eternally separated from Him?"

If necessary, you may wish to establish that our only way of knowing with assurance about the after-life is to search the scriptures. A substitute for the word "DEATH" is *"alienation from God."*

✎ **Jot down below thoughts about SIN and DEATH that you would like to discuss with your partner, or questions you would like answered by your cell leader or pastor:**

_____

_____

_____

_____

_____

Week 3, Day 1
This Unit: Our Mediation
Today: Serving as a Mediator

Read Matthew 10:18-20; Matthew 16:18-19

We seldom use the word "mediator." Yet, it is an important part of life. Webster's dictionary defines this person as: *"One who mediates or interposes between parties at variance for the purpose of reconciling them."* The mediator acts as an agent in a situation where a conflict must be settled.

In Matthew 10:18-20 Jesus said to His disciples,

"On my account you will be brought before governors and kings as witnesses to them and to the Gentiles. But when they arrest you, do not worry about what to say or how to say it. At that time you will be given what to say, for it will not be you speaking, but the Spirit of your Father speaking through you."

As you go to unbelievers, you are participating in an eternal battle being waged for the souls of men. You are a mediator for Christ. Your assignment is to reconcile men to God. Understand that the powers of darkness and the powers of light are in conflict as you seek to mediate, to bring an unbeliever to salvation. All the powers of hell will fight against you!

Sensitivity to the presence of the Holy Spirit is necessary as you witness. He is called the *Paraclete,* a Greek word meaning "one called alongside to help." He will have preceded you into the life of the "Type A" unbeliever, for if it were not for His presence there would be no responsiveness.

Satan will cause all sorts of odd things to happen. For example, through the years there have been scores and scores of times when I had no interruptions when sharing John 3:16 with a seeker. Then, at the *very moment* for the decision for Christ to be made, the baby would scream, the dog would begin to bark, an unexpected visitor would barge in, or the telephone would ring! An unexpected distraction would happen to divert the concentration of the seeker. I concluded years ago that these were never "coincidences." They were the activities of powers of the air who were fighting back!

According to Matthew 10:18-20, who will provide the proper words for you to use when you are witnessing?

☐ The perfectly memorized presentation of John 3:16.

☐ The Holy Spirit, who will inspire your words.

☐ Your persuasive words, sincerely and earnestly spoken.

Be encouraged by this mingling of your spirit with the Spirit of God which will take place as you share with unbelievers.

A TRUE STORY

When planting a church in the Harrisburg area, our family lived across the street from a single man who held wild parties on the weekends. Sometimes naked people would be chasing one another through the snow in his front yard. My sons were small, and this caused many problems for us.

Bob was not yet a "Type A" unbeliever. He was just a hell-raiser! But he needed Jesus. I went over to visit him. His business was to repair kitchen appliances, which he did in the garage of his house. I began to walk over during the weekdays and chat with him. Then Ruth baked an apple pie and gave it to him. Soon we had a good friendship established, and he even tried not to curse in front of me.

Finally, the Lord prompted me to go to his home and ask him to share his past life with me. He had been dumped in an orphanage as a child and had never known a family's love. Entering the army as a youth, he learned to drink and party with men much older than he was.

After further contacts, he asked me to come over and have a cup of coffee with him. Our love had stirred up something within him, and he said, "You know, I'm not much for this religion stuff."

I replied, "Bob, you are 33 years old. Do you ever pray?" He looked at me in astonishment: "I never thought of it!" I said, "That's a shame! Here you are halfway through life and you have never prayed? Would you like me to give you a prayer to say?" He said, "Aw, I don't have anything to say to God. I would only be saying fancy words to make you feel good. No thanks."

At that time you will be given what to say, for it will not be you speaking . . .

I sensed the Holy Spirit's presence as I replied, "No, Bob. I will give you the words of a sincere prayer that really will say where you are spiritually." I had him get down on his knees with me and said, "Now, just repeat these words after me: Dear God *(Dear God),* This is Bob *(This is Bob).* I don't care one thing about you and I don't need you!"

Bob jumped to his feet and said, "I can't say that to God!" I answered, "Bob, do you think you are not speaking those very words to God with every action of your life? Praying does not require you to get on your knees!"

I turned around and walked over to my house. In about an hour, he came over. "Ralph, I think I need for you to talk to me about God!" I am delighted to report to you that Bob not only became a Christian, but went on to serve the Lord with great devotion.

 Meditate today about the way the Holy Spirit cooperates with us as we witness to "Type A" unbelievers. What He guides us to do is often something we would not otherwise say!

Week 3, Day 2

This Unit: Our Mediation

Today: Reconciling Men to God

Read 2 Corinthians 5:15-20

 Carefully read this scripture. Using your pen, <u>underline</u> each phrase that describes our assignment to reconcile men to God:

And he died for all, that those who live should no longer live for themselves but for him who died for them and was raised again. So from now on we regard no one from a worldly point of view. Though we once regarded Christ in this way, we do so no longer. Therefore, if anyone is in Christ, he is a new creation; the old has gone, the new has come! All this is from God, who reconciled us to himself through Christ and gave us the ministry of reconciliation: that God was reconciling the world to himself in Christ, not counting men's sins against them. And he has committed to us the message of reconciliation. We are therefore Christ's ambassadors, as though God were making his appeal through us. We implore you on Christ's behalf: Be reconciled to God.

Mediators are involved in restoring broken relationships between separated parties. Clearly, this scripture calls for us to bring the message of reconciliation to unbelievers.

 Meditate on this John 3:16 presentation for two minutes. Consider the ways it assists you as you participate in your ministry of reconciliation:

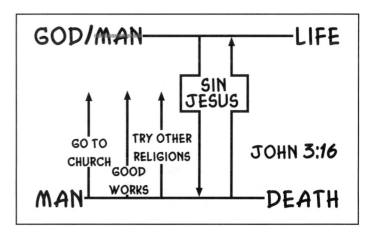

Did you include these thoughts?

1. The very activity of sharing this diagram means you are clearly sharing the *message* of reconciliation.
2. It explains that the relationship with God that has been broken is a choice man has made. It is not God's choice.
3. It rules out all other alternatives but one: Jesus! God has set the terms for us to be reconciled.

60

Could any passage of scripture be more pointed in calling us to be ceaselessly active in bringing unbelievers to Christ? Why do you think so many Christians live irresponsibly, disregarding their mission to be mediators?

A TRUE STORY . . .

A very wealthy church in Richmond, Virginia invited me to share with them about life in the Cell Church. A full presentation was made to the entire congregation, and then we spent another full day with the "pillars" of this church. Some of them had been charter members of the 43-year-old organization. All were pleased by the concept of believers meeting in small groups in homes, and endorsed moving forward into the new model. The pastor was left with a schedule to equip church leaders for the coming transition.

Two months later, he called me late one night. He said, "I have just come from the most shattering session of my ministry. I reviewed the scriptures tonight with my leaders that make it plain that all men, everywhere, who die without coming to Christ to receive salvation from the penalty of sin, are *forever, eternally separated from God.*

"When I finished, I asked for a time of discussion. To my shock, every single church leader in turn said, 'We know that is what the Bible teaches, but we do not believe it. We are confident that God will bring all humanity to Himself, whether or not they come to accept Christ.' "

The pastor said, "I always *assumed* that this basic teaching of scripture was not questioned by the leadership here. Now I realize that the problem I face is not transitioning a church structure, but confronting powerful unbelief and apostasy among my church leaders."

What about your own convictions? Have you clearly settled for yourself that the cross proves man can be forever separated from God? Thoughtfully review the following scriptures. <u>Underline</u> the phrases that affirm we are to be reconcilers:

Not only is this so, but we also rejoice in God through our Lord Jesus Christ, through whom we have now received reconciliation. (Romans 5:11)

For he himself is our peace, who has made the two one and has destroyed the barrier, the dividing wall of hostility, by abolishing in his flesh the law with its commandments and regulations. His purpose was to create in himself one new man out of the two, thus making peace, and in this one body to reconcile both of them to God through the cross, by which he put to death their hostility. He came and preached peace to you who were far away and peace to those who were near. (Ephesians 2:14-17)

. . . and through him to reconcile to himself all things, whether things on earth or things in heaven, by making peace through his blood, shed on the cross. (Colossians 1:20)

Week 3, Day 3
This Unit: Our Mediation
Today: Peter, The Mediator

Read Acts 10:28-33

There are two powerful illustrations in the book of Acts for you to discover how God will use you in your ministry to "Type A" unbelievers. If you have time, it would be worthwhile to read the entire passage from Acts 9:43-10:44, which tells the story of the first of them. It narrates how God arranged for a "Type A" seeker to be converted by Peter.

In Caesarea, a Roman official named Cornelius was sincerely searching for God. He lived in a Roman colony, the governmental headquarters of the region.

Cornelius was the classic "Man of Peace!" He had searched for the living God for some time, and had demonstrated his desire to follow Him by doing many benevolent acts.

It was three o'clock in the afternoon when an angel appeared to him and told him to send for Peter, who was in Joppa. The exact location of the apostle was described by the angel. *Note that Cornelius required God's mediator, Peter, before he could be saved.*

Meanwhile, 35 miles to the south along the seacoast, Peter had to be prepared for this encounter. A strict Jew, Peter would never have spoken about Christ to a Roman soldier.

He was still living in the bondage of Judaism, not yet free to go to non-Jews with the message of salvation.

God dealt with him at noonday as he sunned himself on the flat rooftop of Simon's house. He saw a vision of animals that were not *kosher* for a Jew, coming down from the sky on a large sheet. The Lord's voice commanded him to eat the flesh of these animals. He was shocked! He used two words that cannot ever be put together in the same sentence: "No, Lord!" (To say "Lord," there must never be a "No!" Only a "Yes" goes with "Lord.") For emphasis, the vision was repeated three times.

Soon after, the centurion's servants came to guide Peter over the 30 mile road which ran along the side of the Mediterranean Sea to their master's house. Upon arriving, Peter experienced the most profound activity of God. Not only Cornelius but all in his *oikos* were saved and filled with the Holy Spirit.

GOD JOINS US TO SEEKING UNBELIEVERS

As you begin your ministry to "Type A" unbelievers, be very sure that when you find a "Man of Peace" you did not get there first! The Holy Spirit of God arrived in advance of you. At the same time He is enlarging your own vision of what He desires to do through you, He is preparing the soil of human hearts who are searching for Christ!

You will probably be surprised the first few times this happens to you. You will help someone pray to receive Christ and think, "I never knew it could be that easy."

A TRUE STORY

When planting a church in Middletown, Pennsylvania, I used to get my fuel at the same station each few days. Usually there were many cars being serviced, and the station manager was always rushing from one to the next. Nevertheless, I took time to visit with him as he filled up my tank. We learned a little bit about each other's families, but there did not seem to be a desire on his part to get involved with a pastor.

One night as I was praying, the Lord said to me, "Get dressed and go the the service station where you get gas. You need to speak to the manager about his soul!"

I said, "Lord, it's late. He's probably closing up about now. He will think it strange that I would appear for no good reason. I will see him tomorrow."

"No!" said the Lord. "Go now."

Obediently, I dressed and drove 15 minutes to the station. As I suspected, the lights had been turned off and he was filling out the daily report in his office. I walked in and said, "This may be inconvenient for you, but the Lord told me to come to you and ask one question; "Is it well with your soul?"

He began to weep profusely. "No," he said, "It's not! I have just learned I have an incurable cancer and I will have to stop working here very shortly. Pastor, for the past few days as I have filled up your car with gas I have prayed, 'God, this man always seems to be in a hurry. I don't want to bother him, but I'm scared. I don't know much about You. Please, God, make him aware I need him to help me!"

Now it was my turn to weep! I had been so busy with my own church affairs I had delayed seeking to relate deeply to this man. The Holy Spirit had repeated the same scenario that took place in Joppa and Caesarea centuries ago. I ministered to that man in the months that followed, preached his funeral, and saw his entire family come to know the Lord.

NOW, IT'S YOUR TURN TO WEEP . . .

He who goes out weeping, carrying seed to sow, will return with songs of joy, carrying sheaves with him. (Psalm 126:6)

In your cell group, you have already learned that *edification* takes place when you hear the need in the life of your fellow Christian and then hear Christ. You have experienced receiving from Him what will bless others. This same communication with Christ in your prayer life will cause you to feel a "tap on the shoulder," as He says to you, "Go *now* to speak to your unbelieving friend." When you arrive, you will discover an openness that has been caused by the activity of the Holy Spirit.

This ministry to the "pre-Christian" "Type A" unbeliever is a *supernatural* activity. Be sensitive to the Lord's voice. After one or two personal experiences of your own, you will never be the same! Your life will be enriched by seeing the harvest.

Week 3, Day 4
This Unit: Our Mediation
Today: Philip, the Mediator

Read Acts 8:26-39

Many scriptures tell us that Jesus is the only mediator between God and man:

> For there is one God and one mediator between God and men, the man Christ Jesus, who gave himself as a ransom for all men—the testimony given in its proper time. (1 Timothy 2:5-6)

That Mediator, Christ, dwells in you! He will flow through you with all His love and compassion as you yield yourself to Him.

But there's more! There is also the mediating work of the Holy Spirit taking place in the Man of Peace. Jesus said:

> But I tell you the truth: It is for your good that I am going away. Unless I go away, the Counselor will not come to you; but if I go, I will send him to you. When he comes, he will convict the world of guilt in regard to sin and righteousness and judgment: in regard to sin, because men do not believe in me; in regard to righteousness, because I am going to the Father,

where you can see me no longer; and in regard to judgment, because the prince of this world now stands condemned. (John 16:7-11)

 How many truths does the Holy Spirit speak into the Man of Peace before you arrive? <u>Underline</u> in the previous passage the truths He reveals.

Did you underline three? You will be the *second* person, not the *first*, to discuss sin, righteousness, and judgment. You may be sure the Holy Spirit has already been revealing these matters to the unbeliever. Jesus taught:

> "I tell you the truth, no one can enter the kingdom of God unless he is born of water and the Spirit." (John 3:5)

The word "convict" means "to bring to light, to expose." Before any person can become a Christian, the Holy Spirit must come and speak.

Are there some who are *not ever called by Him?* No! God is not willing that *any* should perish, so the Spirit comes to all men (2 Peter 3:9).

ANOTHER EXAMPLE OF A "MAN OF PEACE"

The record of Philip and a eunuch from Ethiopia is another classic example of the way people are prepared for your coming to them. The eunuch had come a long distance seeking God's presence. He had to travel all the way from North Africa, but would never be received into the Jewish religion because he was a eunuch, and being able to procreate was a requirement for proselytes.

He was seeking after truth, reading the story of the suffering servant in Isaiah 53. Sadly, he had to return home without finding the rest for his soul he had come so far to receive.

The Holy Spirit, who had been working in his life, knew that if he returned to the paganism of Queen Candace's court he would *never* find salvation! As in the case of Peter and Cornelius, the scripture reveals an angel of the Lord appeared and gives instructions to Philip. The supernatural activity of God is again the source of the encounter between these two men.

Philip would have felt like a fool standing along a dusty road except for one thing: *he knew he was sent by God.* He did not know why he was there when he got there. Obedience to the calling of the Spirit always precedes ministry.

When the Ethiopian appeared, he was diligently reading a valuable hand-written scroll of Isaiah. This was not a small document, nor was it an inexpensive item. Clinging to hope, he was seeking to discover what the writing taught.

You will discover among those called the "Man of Peace" some who have already started to read the scriptures. In their search, many are victimized by the cults, who focus on being "experts" at what the Bible teaches (along with their other spurious books). It is with such persons the *investigative Bible study materials* will be of great assistance.

So it was that Philip boarded the chariot and rode farther and farther in the wrong direction from his home. No amount of inconvenience in getting back would deter him from having this "investigative Bible study" with the eunuch!

The account concludes with the confession of faith by the eunuch, his baptism by immersion in a river beside the road, and his going on his way rejoicing.

NOTE THE IMPACT UPON PHILIP

The next information we are given about this man is that he has gone to evangelize the neglected area of Samaria, and his daughters have joined him in his ministry. Beware! When you discover the partnership you have with the Holy Spirit, as the Christ within you becomes the Mediator through your life, your entire future may be revised. This is the wonderful thing that happens to obedient Christians.

One day, perhaps sooner than you think, the Holy Spirit may call you to serve in a greater capacity. After you have harvested your first "Man of Peace," He will propel you into the world of those who seem to be Christ-rejecters!

REMINDER
You and your partner should take time to report to your cell group about the contacts you are making. Seek their prayer support.
If there are any "Men of Peace" in their oikoses you might visit, get their names.

Week 3, Day 5
This Unit: Our Mediation
Today: Review John 3:16 Diagram

Read Ephesians 2:8-9; Philippians 3:4-9; 2:5-11

GOD/~~MAN~~————————LIFE

SIN

MAN————————DEATH

STEP 8:
This line represents our daily life being lived apart from the plan God has for us. The heartache inside and outside us in the world is the result of rejecting His guidance.

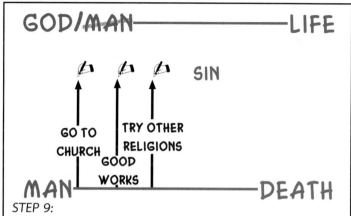

GOD/MAN————————LIFE

SIN

GO TO CHURCH · GOOD WORKS · TRY OTHER RELIGIONS

MAN————————DEATH

STEP 9:
Knowing something is wrong, we try to get back to God without returning the ownership of our life to Him. We try to get back to him by going to church. We think doing good works may help. We even try other religions or cults. Nothing works! We stubbornly insist on controlling our lives.

Ephesians 2:8-9 documents the above. Write below a comment you might make when explaining how man lives seeking to add merit to his self-owned life:

_____

_____

_____

Meditate on Paul's words in Philippians 3:4-9. How could you paraphrase them when adding the three elements shown above to your diagram?

_____

_____

_____

_____

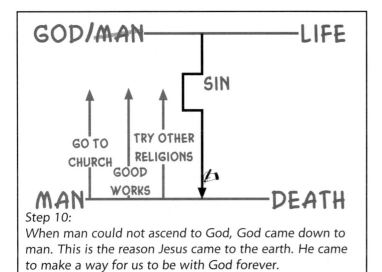

Step 10:

When man could not ascend to God, God came down to man. This is the reason Jesus came to the earth. He came to make a way for us to be with God forever.

Think about this great truth! Christ came to redeem us! Ponder over Philippians 2:5-11. What does the Holy Spirit inspire you to share about the coming of Christ to the earth with "Type A" unbelievers?

_____

_____

_____

_____

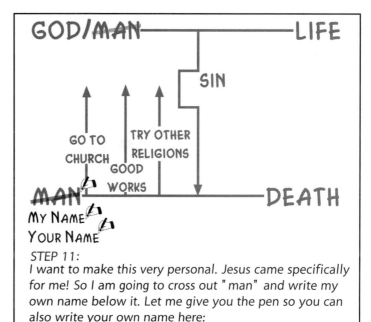

STEP 11:

I want to make this very personal. Jesus came specifically for me! So I am going to cross out "man" and write my own name below it. Let me give you the pen so you can also write your own name here:

Many times we miss the *application* of a truth by not making it personal. Writing both your names in the way shown above may seem to you to be rather childish. You will no longer think about it that way after you have actually done it a few times with a "Type A" unbeliever!

It is important that as you share this part of the diagram, you have a strong awareness of the Holy Spirit's anointing upon you. Christ will be present as you write your names.

WEEK 4, DAY 1
THIS UNIT: OUR MOTIVE
TODAY: WHY DO YOU GO?

Read 2 Timothy 1:8-13

A *motive,* according to the dictionary, refers to "that which determines the choice or moves the will." This week, we are going to think about your motives for touching the lost with your life. How long will this equipping course be used by you?

Since 1950, many subgroups within the Christian world have offered training for reaching the lost. Many books have been written about how to evangelize. *Yet, fewer than 5% of those in the traditional church have ever sought to reach unbelievers.* Years ago I wrote a book entitled "Target Group Evangelism." It sold poorly and went out of print. My publisher then said, "Your *title* killed the book. Christians do not buy books about "evangelism." If you had left that word out of the title, it would have had many readers."

A TRUE STORY . . .

I spoke in Suffolk, Virginia to a church about the priority of reaching the lost. A lady requested a private visit with me in her home. I entered a stately mansion with the finest of Chippendale furniture and was served tea by her maid. She stood by the windows that overlooked the street and said, "I was born in this house and raised my three daughters here. I now live alone." Choking with emotion, she said, "To my knowledge, all the people who live in these houses surrounding mine have *never* attended a church. I was careful to help my own children come to Christ, but I have never spoken to another person in this world about their spiritual need. I am so ashamed! *Is it too late for me to seek to reach those who have lived beside me for all these years?"*

WHAT IS *YOUR* MOTIVE FOR REACHING THE LOST?

The Faith Community Baptist Church in Singapore, a fully developed Cell Church, has 7,000 attending as this is being written. A survey revealed that nearly 65% of the cell group members now lead others to Christ! In 1996, 1,800 of these cell members will spend a month at their own expense in evangelism teams working will Cell Churches in other nations. This reveals their high priority for reaching the lost.

The 80,000 Cell members of the *Eglise Protestante Baptiste Oeuvres et Mission* in Abidjan, Ivory Coast are so motivated to reach the lost that their cell groups multiply *every four months*.

You are a part of the Cell Church movement that has spread across the world, and is the fastest growing segment of Christianity today. Those Cell members who have put reaching the lost as one of their highest priorities are regularly seeing conversions as they reach out. During this segment of the *Year of Equipping* training, it is important for

THE NATURAL WORLD FOR NATURAL PERSONS

I CORINTHIANS 2:14: "A man who is unspiritual refuses what belongs to the Spirit of God..."

SELF-CENTERED
HEARS NATURAL SOUNDS
SEES PHYSICAL OBJECTS
FILLED WITH PRIDE
SMELLS NATURAL ODORS
LOVES WITH HUMAN LOVE

MANY TALENTS

SKILLS
ABILITIES
STRENGTHS

THE SPIRITUAL WORLD FOR SPIRITUAL PERSONS

I CORINTHIANS 2:15: "A man gifted with the Spirit can judge the worth of everything..."

IS FILLED WITH COMPASSION
HEARS SPIRITUAL SOUNDS
SEES SPIRITUAL TRUTHS
HAS SPIRITUAL BOLDNESS
SENSES THINGS OF THE SPIRIT
LOVES WITH CHRIST'S LOVE

MANY GIFTS

SERVING
GIVING   DISCERNING
FAITH   TRUE/FALSE
PROPHECY   SPIRITS
WISE   TEACHING
  SPEECH   ETC.

you to decide whether you will join their number as a servant of Christ who will prioritize reaching the lost *for the rest of your life.*

WHY DO WE GO?

There are "Men of Peace" around us at all times. Jesus was burdened for his blind disciples who could not see the "whitened fields," and often took them where they would meet needy lives. In Samaria, they could not see the people who were looking for Jesus, so He demonstrated their presence by ministering to the woman at the well. He said to them, *"I have food to eat that you know nothing about" (John 4:32).*

As you complete this fourth week of your journey into reaching "Type A" unbelievers, consider God's assignment for each of His children to bring the unreached to Him. Let Paul's words go with you as you leave today's Daily Growth Guide:

So do not be ashamed to testify about our Lord . . . . But join with me in suffering for the gospel, by the power of God, who has saved us and called us to a holy life—not because of anything we have done but because of his own purpose and grace. . . . And of this gospel I was appointed a herald and an apostle and a teacher. That is why I am suffering as I am. Yet I am not ashamed, because I know whom I have believed, and am convinced that he is able to guard what I have entrusted to him for that day. What you heard from me, keep as the pattern of sound teaching, with faith and love in Christ Jesus. (2 Timothy 1:8-13)

 Is the Lord placing a name of an unbeliever in your mind at this moment? If so, write it here:

_____

69

Week 4, Day 2
This Unit: Our Motive
Today: Why Did Jesus Go?

Read John 4:34-37; 18:37; 2 Peter 3:9

Motive: "that which determines the choice or moves the will." When we lived according to the standards of this world, we freely chose to do what pleased us. When we realize that Christ dwells within us, seeking to do His work through our lives, we are to offer the parts of our bodies to Him as "instruments of righteousness"(Romans 6:13). His choice must become our choice.

What motivated Jesus' choices? Why did He come to earth? What motivated Him to spend time with winebibbers and sinners? What caused Him to spend whole nights in prayer as He wept over Jerusalem?

What motivated Him? *Whatever* motivated Him brought Him from heaven to earth! Consider Philippians 2:6-8:

> *. . . being in very nature God, did not consider equality with God something to be grasped, but made himself nothing, taking the very nature of a servant, being made in human likeness. And being found in appearance as a man, he humbled himself and became obedient to death—even death on a cross!*

These words of His capture His motive for us:

> *. . . Jesus answered, "You are right in saying I am a king. In fact, for this reason I was born, and for this I came into the world, to testify to the truth."* (John 18:37)

Think as you read these words today: *this very same Christ lives in you!* His motives today are identical to what they were when He dwelled in the body given to Him by the Father and Mary—but now He dwells in *you*.

He looks at the sordid mess people make of their lives. He sees the battered wife and the drug-filled youth. He watches the greed of government agents who steal from the public in the same way as did the tax collectors of His time. He sees the poor, the oppressed, the demon-possessed, the prisoners of today. What is His attitude toward them?

> *The Lord is not slow in keeping his promise, as some understand slowness. He is patient with you, not wanting anyone to perish, but everyone to come to repentance.* (2 Peter 3:9)

Ask yourself: if Christ lived in your family, performed the same daily duties you do, faced the same struggles you have, what would He be like? How would He use His days?

Of course, *He does all that,* for He lives in you. How clearly have we allowed His motives to be pressed over our own? It is interesting that Christ had angry, judgmental words to say to the religious leaders of His day, but only words of compassion for the people whose lives were messed up. He said to the prostitute, "Go and sin no more." He said to the woman at the well, "You have been divorced five times and now live with another man." He said to the crooked, scheming tax collector, "Zacchaeus, . . . I must stay at your house today" (Luke 19:5).

Over and over again, we see Jesus motivated by love for those who were deceived by Satan, whose lives were filled with wretchedness. His pity for the fallen never caused Him to condemn them. His condemnation was saved for the proud Pharisees, the religious leaders. *This is the Christ who lives in you!*

A TRUE STORY . . .

Many years ago, I read a book titled *The Witness* by Urie Bender.* It spoke of the great need for Christians to become involved in the lives of unbelievers. I was so impressed with it that I contacted his publisher, located him, and flew to Michigan to visit him.

Urie had been a high level denominational leader among the Mennonites. He was travelling the earth in his ministry, but had a gnawing feeling he was not really living as Jesus lived. He resigned his job and went to a factory in Indiana that manufactured mobile homes. He explained to the personnel director that his credentials should be ignored, and

that he just wanted to be hired as a worker on the assembly line. He asked that his former identity not be revealed to anyone.

Day after day, he worked beside the cursing, lust-filled men and women in that factory. Daily he prayed, "Christ in me, show me how You would touch these people." Eating lunch, working beside them, listening to their problems, he gradually began to see a radical change in their attitude toward him. One woman, pregnant with an illegitimate child, sought his counsel. An alcoholic middle-aged man asked for his encouragement. One by one, the people on that assembly line were impacted by his life.

The Christ within Him had been fully released to reveal Himself, and the result was a changed factory. The experience caused Bender to take a small inheritance and purchase a motel near a small town, where he would have time to pray, to write books, and to minister to others.

As you have read today's thoughts, what are your own thoughts? What major and minor revisions of your lifestyle is Christ calling to you to make, so He can be more free to place you in the path of seeking people He desires to meet and redeem?

_____

_____

_____

_____

---

* Now out of print.

71

WEEK 4, DAY 3
THIS UNIT: OUR MOTIVE
TODAY: WHY DID PAUL GO?

Read Acts 20:21-24; 2 Timothy 4:5-8

Saul of Tarsus went totally blind during his conversion experience. When the scales finally fell away from his eyes, he saw the world in a radically different way. In his personal letters to his co-workers, he never mentions the sights to see when visiting a city, or the best place to get fried fish. He did not speak of the things travellers usually discuss. His only thoughts were for the souls of men. He had lost his life to find it again!

This man's motives make up large portions of his writings. He gives his passionate appeal to us in Acts 20:21:

I have declared to both Jews and Greeks that they must turn to God in repentance and have faith in our Lord Jesus.

His conduct was always guided by the Holy Spirit. He spent much time seeking direction for his life and ministry. As one reads his writings, again and again he refers in passing to the way he followed the Spirit's directions:

And now, compelled by the Spirit, I am going to Jerusalem, not knowing what will happen to me there. I only know that in every city the Holy Spirit warns me that prison and hardships are facing me. However, I consider my life worth nothing to me, if only I may finish the race and complete the task the Lord Jesus has given me—the task of testifying to the gospel of God's grace. (Acts 20:22-24)

As did the religious establishment with Jesus, so they persecuted Paul wherever he went. He was the brunt of beatings and even stonings by them.

As did Jesus, he spent His time among the people who lived in darkness. He made tents in order to have contacts with people in a new city. He sought out the oppressed in Ephesus and caused so many conversions he bankrupted the idol manufacturing industry. What motivated him?

Paul had met Jesus in an encounter that would shake his values to the core. After going to cell groups meeting in the homes of Jerusalem and dragging adults off to jail as their terrified children watched, he observed Stephen being stoned to death at his direction. The glow of heaven on his face, Stephen asked God to forgive his murderers.

Paul had a clear understanding of what he was capable of doing in his own flesh. It bothered him greatly! He felt like he had goads stuck into his flesh, torn within by the memories of the violence and death he had done to others. When He met Christ, there was a complete cleansing of his soul.

Motivated by his new relationship with the Lord, he gave us his philosophy of life in Galatians 2:20:

I have been crucified with Christ and I no longer live, but Christ lives in me. The life I live in the body, I live by faith in the Son of God, who loved me and gave himself for me.

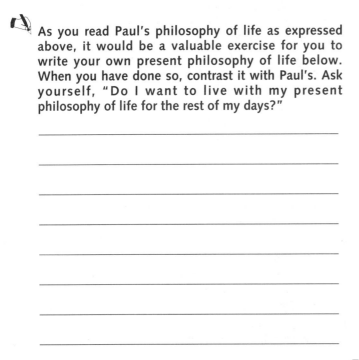 As you read Paul's philosophy of life as expressed above, it would be a valuable exercise for you to write your own present philosophy of life below. When you have done so, contrast it with Paul's. Ask yourself, "Do I want to live with my present philosophy of life for the rest of my days?"

_____

_____

_____

_____

_____

_____

PAUL'S REVIEW OF HIS LIFE

After spending a lifetime serving the Lord as a Cell Church planter across Asia Minor, Paul was finally arrested and sent to Rome. There he lived under house arrest. His reflections during the hours before he was martyred by being burned alive give us insights into his life's motives:

. . . the time has come for my departure. I have fought the good fight, I have finished the race, I have kept the faith. Now there is in store for me the crown of righteousness, which the Lord, the righteous Judge, will award to me on that day—and not only to me, but also to all who have longed for his appearing. (2 Timothy 4:5-8)

Here is a tombstone. Imagine it is yours. If it were Paul's, it would probably read, "I have fought the good fight." What would you like to write on yours?

Week 4, Day 4
This Unit: Our Motive
Today: Who Do We Reveal?

Read Galatians 2:20

A famous Chinese Christian, Watchman Nee, said that when he realized he was in Christ, he was filled with great joy. But, he went on to say, when it dawned on him that Christ was in *him,* he became so excited he ran down the street of his village crying, "Christ lives in me! Christ lives in me!"

Reaching "Type A" unbelievers is simply a matter of getting close enough to them for the Christ in you to be revealed. There are so many ways He speaks through us; the problem is our self-centered lifestyles insulate Him from the people He would like to meet, heal, and deliver.

Our motive for living should be to serve as Christ's "delivery system," bringing Him into the places He enjoys to meet the people He loves. As we have already learned, the Holy Spirit has preceded us, conviction of sin, righteousness, and judgment. The Father has revealed Himself through the creation He has made (Romans 1). The Son came to earth to atone for all our sins. *The missing piece hindering a mighty harvest is where we take these bodies of ours that are inhabited by His wonderful presence.*

A STORY FROM CHINA

The trains in China have narrow compartments where people sit facing each other with a table between them. One day a Christian entered the train and sat across from a stranger.

As the train pulled out of the station, the stranger pulled out a bottle of strong spirits and a deck of cards. "It will be a thirty-hour trip for us to take together. Let's use the time to drink and gamble!"

Courteously, the Christian bowed to him and said, "Oh, I am so sorry, sir. I cannot join you. You see, I do not have my *hands* with me."

The man looked surprised and confused. The Christian's hands were clearly visible. After a moment, the Christian continued: "Oh, you see *these* hands. Naturally, you think they belong to me, but they do not. You see, some time ago I realized that I had stolen my life from its rightful owner. I admitted that God has the right to own me. I tried and tried to get to Him, but nothing I did made it happen. Then I discovered that all the time I was seeking Him, He had already come to seek me. He sent His son Jesus to this earth, and He took my stolen life to a cross. There He died as my substitute, paying the penalty for the theft of my life. When I discovered this, I said, 'Jesus, take my life. I give it to you to control.' From that day to this, these hands have belong to Him. They do his work, and I have no more rights to do with them as I desire. And He has never desired to use them to gamble or drink. So you see, I am quite helpless to join you. Please, sir, excuse me. *I do not have my hands with me.*"

THE PRIMARY MOTIVATION OF THE CHRISTIAN LIFE

Why should we decide, once and for all, that we will offer ourselves as a living sacrifice to Christ? It is because He alone can satisfy our desire to live a meaningful existence, one that will have eternal meaning.

Of course, we should have a deep-as-life motivation to see unbelievers join us in the family of God. *Of course,* we desire for the Kingdom of God to increase and for our cell group to multiply again and again as we reap the harvest.

But these are secondary to the basic value of the Christian: *to know God, and enjoy Him forever.* This, as a theologian wrote many years ago, is "the chief end of man."

A TRUE STORY . . .

George was raised in a Polish family. As he says, "To be Polish is to be a Catholic." He grew up in the church, faithfully attending with his father and mother. He explains, "All my life I was told that God would not love me until I merited His love. I was led to believe He disliked me because of my sins, and would never accept me into heaven until I became good enough to stand before Him."

Perhaps *you* have lived with that same belief system. Have you also felt unworthy, that God would never use a person with your spiritual "warts and pimples?"

He became an accountant in London, England, and was involved with a Christian who worked for him. Gently, this man lived the life of a committed believer. He never pushed, never pressured the message of Christ. Gradually, the relationship deepened and George began to ask questions. His friend gave him a small Bible, which he threw in his suitcase. A few weeks went by. George thought, "I am an ungrateful person: this man was kind enough to give this book to me. I should at least read it."

He began to read in Matthew, Acts, and Romans. As he further discussed the life of Jesus with his friend, he was overwhelmed with a great truth: *God loved him as he was!*

He describes his conversion experience: "There I was, on a commuter train in London, with people all around me. I sat alone, thinking about this great truth. God loved me just exactly like I was so much that He gave His only son to bring me to Him. I began to silently weep, the tears running down my cheeks. It was a wonderful moment, the moment of my new birth."

THE WHOLE PROCESS YOU ARE LEARNING TOOK PLACE!

George was a potential "Man of Peace," a part of the whitened fields that were not harvested. God placed a believer in his path, who carefully revealed the indwelling Christ. There followed the discussions, an investigative Bible study period, and finally that powerful moment at the Cross, which happened on a commuter train! *It is my prayer as you finish today's materials you will say, "Lord! Do it again!"*

Week 4, Day 5
This Unit: Our Motive
Today: Review John 3:16 Diagram

Read 2 Corinthians 6:2

What words would be appropriate for *you* to speak here?

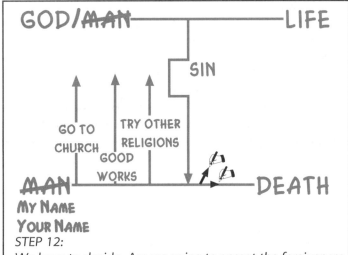

STEP 12:
We have to decide. Are we going to accept the forgiveness God has offered us when Jesus paid for our sins by His death on the cross, or are we going to continue to live an independent life of our own?

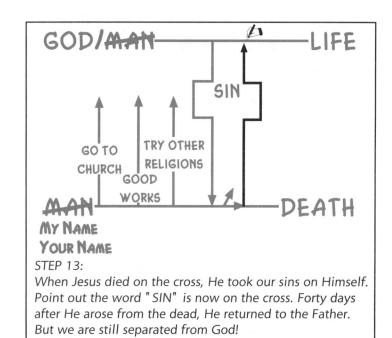

STEP 13:
When Jesus died on the cross, He took our sins on Himself. Point out the word "SIN" is now on the cross. Forty days after He arose from the dead, He returned to the Father. But we are still separated from God!

Meditate on 2 Corinthians 6:2 as you examine these panels for Steps 12 and 13. How can you personalize what you are going to say when sharing these truths?

_____

_____

_____

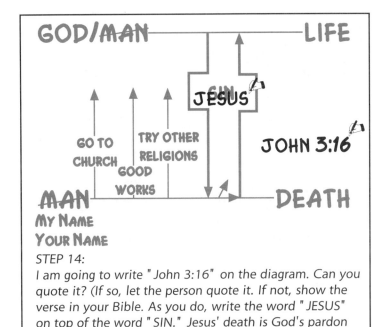

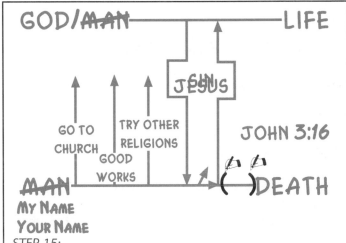

STEP 14:
I am going to write "John 3:16" on the diagram. Can you quote it? (If so, let the person quote it. If not, show the verse in your Bible. As you do, write the word "JESUS" on top of the word "SIN." Jesus' death is God's pardon for our sin.

STEP 15:
Draw a bracket on the bottom line and say, "If we take the way of the cross back to God, we give up the rights to our own lives. He is given back His rightful place. This is what it costs us all to follow Jesus."

It is appropriate to have a small pocket sized New Testament with you when you share with an unbeliever. You can turn to it as you come to Step 14. If the unbeliever cannot quote the verse, listen as they read it aloud.

What points will you make as you overwrite the word "JESUS" on top of the word "SIN?" Share how He became our substitute, taking our sin, giving us simultaneously His life.

This should make a powerful impact upon the person! You are not just offering an "eternal life assurance policy!" You are saying, "Beginning here and now, this commitment means you invite Jesus Christ to become your master." Do you remember the word *pais*, explained in *The Arrival Kit*? To become a *child* of God is to become a *servant* of God at the same time. Declaring Christ as Lord is not a "second step" in the Christian life; it is the *first step*. Before asking the unbeliever to pray, talk this through in dialogue together.

WEEK 5, DAY 1
THIS UNIT: OUR MINISTRY
TODAY: INVESTIGATIVE BIBLE STUDIES

Read Hebrews 11:6

A TRUE STORY

He was a student in the University of Singapore when a new friend asked him about his religious beliefs. "I'm a freethinker," he said. "I don't believe any religion is worth my time. I'm here to make a fortune and enjoy life."

This same man is now a Zone Pastor in the Faith Community Baptist Church! What happened to him? How did he find Christ?

"My friend did not try to argue with me. Instead, he became a true companion. We studied together, we played squash together, we went camping together. His life made a real impact on me. I respected him."

It was then this Christian said to him, "Would it not be terrible if truth about God existed, and you never discovered it? An atheist is someone who says, 'There is no god!' But an agnostic says, 'I do not *know* if there is a god.' An honest agnostic will be open to further search for God. I believe that's where you are. Am I right?"

78

STUDY GUIDE TWELVE: THAT PRECIOUS BLOOD

A woman began to cheat on her husband. When they moved to another town, she returned to being faithful to him. She could not forgive herself for what she had done. In the months that followed, she developed many physical problems. Doctors suggested her ailments were induced by her inner conflicts. She could not bring herself to admit to anyone what she had done. As the years passed, she became bedridden.

12-1 Her physical problems occurred because she was unable to
f _orgive_ **herself.**

A man committed murder while drunk. He spent 5 years in prison. His debt to society was paid. Twenty years later, he said, "My stay in prison was not long enough to make me feel I'm forgiven. I still feel guilty for what I did. I guess I'll never be free again!"

12-2 What was his problem? (✓ your answer)
- ☑ **A. His prison sentence was too short.**
- ☒ **B. He could not forgive himself for his crime.**
- ☐ **C. He was afraid he might do it again.**

Self-punishment is never enough to cancel out our wrongs, is it? It is not possible for us to simply forgive ourselves for what we have done in the past. We know that wrongs must be punished, and the punishment must fit the wrong. Therefore, we constantly live with the weight of personal guilt. Can anything be done?

In ancient times, a person would take a lamb to the priest, lay a hand on it, and confess wrong doings. That animal became a substitute for the sinning person. It would then be sacrificed. By its death, it took the judgment for the evildoer's wrong doings. The death of the animal made it possible for the person to be forgiven.

12-1: forgive. 12-2: B

"I guess so," said the freethinker. "What do you have in mind?"

In the weeks that followed, the two of them met to share a Bible study to examine its teachings about God. "At first, I was doing the study to be polite to my friend. But gradually I began to realize there was a whole area of truth I had ignored. After the sixth week, I began to truly search for God. When I understood about the death of God's Son, I knew I could never walk away and reject Christ again!"

USE INVESTIGATIONAL BIBLE STUDIES AT LEVEL 2

If needed, review the simple instructions on pages 31-32 which explain the procedure. The advice given there is the result of many experiences others have had when conducting investigational Bible studies with searching unbelievers.

Here are some other tips that will help you:

1. Does the unbeliever own a Bible? If so, ask where it came from. It may have sentimental value. For example, one "Type A" unbeliever said, "I own a Bible. It was my grandmother's. It was given to me at her funeral." Its pages were worn from use. God had allowed it to fall into the hands of a grandchild to be a link of faith. Honor its use as you study together.

2. If the unbeliever does not own a Bible, purchase one with a quality binding and present it as a gift. Write a brief note in the presentation page with your name and date on it. Let it become a link between *your* faith and the searching heart of your friend.

3. Look at the reduced page shown to the left. Note that the blank has been filled in and the proper box has been checked. People retain 60% more by interacting physically with the questions in the material. Therefore, you should present a fresh copy of the booklet to your friend, but have your own copy already filled in from your personal study of the materials. Explain, "The value of writing in the answers provides better understanding of the truths presented."

4. *Do not gloss over the cartoons.* While the Bible studies provide the knowledge that is lacking, each cartoon offers a way of discussing the inner feelings of the unbeliever. For example, when referring to the one shown on page 78, you might say, "I count myself among those who felt like this cartoon character. I was always running, but had no purpose for my life. Have you ever felt that way?" The resulting conversation may open new areas for you to discuss.

Before you leave this page, jot down what the Holy Spirit has been saying to you about a friend who needs you to offer this investigational Bible study:

NAME OF PERSON: _____

WHAT I WILL DO NOW: _____

_____

_____

_____

WEEK 5, DAY 2
THIS UNIT: OUR MINISTRY
TODAY: HANDLING EXCUSES 1

Read Matthew 20:25-28

As you finish sharing the John 3:16 presentation, a few persons may respond with excuses for not accepting Christ as their Savior and Lord. Knowing how to deal with them in advance will help you to be more effective in your harvesting ministry.

 Review pages 29-30, "HOW TO HANDLE EXCUSES," before reading today's material.

First, let's consider some ways that will *not* work when handling excuses. These are the "Ping-Pong Method" and the "Great Debate Method." The Christian who uses them is not flowing with Christ's love, seeking instead to overpower.

ABOUT THE "PING-PONG" METHOD . . .

Using this method, you begin to trade answers about the excuse: you answer the excuse, the person answers your answer, you answer that answer.......until someone drops the ball. There follows a moment of mutual embarrassment!

Even using scripture to answer an excuse may be incorporated as a part of the "Ping-Pong" method. It will have little effect without the convicting work of the Holy Spirit.

ABOUT THE "GREAT DEBATE" METHOD . . .

This method pits the intellectual prowess of each person against the other. The *excuse* causes the Christian to quote sources and use logic to overpower the other person. Instead of achieving this objective, the *excuse-giver* draws upon still other sources, uses "better" logic, and the debate is on. Unfortunately, there is no jury to decide who has the better case. The situation deteriorates, hostility arises, and the opportunity to share in the future is destroyed.

Avoid this method at all costs. Excuses are never intended to be answered. They are a polite way to say, "No, thank you!" An excuse-maker is embarrassed when the other person is not quick enough to recognize this, and keeps insisting the excuse is unsatisfactory.

EXAMPLE:

A farmer was asked one day by his neighbor to loan him a rake. He replied, "I can't. I'm going to town!" His wife overheard his reply. After the neighbor had left the area, she said, "That was silly! How can you use the rake if you're going to town?" He replied with a grin, "When you don't want to loan your rake, one excuse is as good as another!"

AVOID THESE FIRST TWO METHODS!

You may triumph in the discussion over the other person, but you will never reach the unbeliever for our Lord. There is a better way. It is the way of the "servant-Christian" (Matthew 20:25-28). Respect the dignity of the other person, and share in a way that is sensitive to the activity of the Holy Spirit.

Let's look at it...

The only sensible way to handle excuses is not to answer them at all! Instead, seek to determine the real issue which has prompted the excuse.

EXAMPLES:

Excuse: "I don't understand enough about the Bible to make a decision like this. I want more time to study before making up my mind."

Answer: "Would it help you to share with me the conditions which hindered you from reading the Bible in the past?"

Excuse: "This is really interesting, but I want to be by myself when I do this..."

Answer: "Can you share with me why being alone when you do this is important to you?"

PROBE! ASK QUESTIONS!

Seek to find the underlying basis for this camouflage!

FIVE PROBE PRINCIPLES

1. DELIBERATE - DON'T DEBATE
   When an excuse is given, probe by asking a question instead of giving a rebuttal: "When did you begin to feel that way?"

2. BE TENDER - NOT TRAUMATIC
   Your gentle spirit will be a foundation for the Holy Spirit to minister to the deep need in this life. Having an argumentative spirit will trigger defensiveness in the other person.

3. CONVERSE - DON'T CONFRONT
   Avoid confrontation! Study the tactful way Jesus did this in His conversation with the woman in Samaria in John 4:1-26.

4. RESPECT - DON'T REJECT
   Lost persons often feel their lack of faith excludes them from being accepted by those who have faith. If your friend feels you consider yourself "better" or "superior" because you have become a Christian, your ministry will be lost. If you show respect and treat the other person as having infinite worth, you will be given the same respect.

5. LOVE - LOVE - LOVE!
   "If you cut me up into a hundred pieces, every one would cry out, 'I love you! I love you! I love you!'" These words, spoken by a Christian to a drug addict brandishing a long switchblade, caused the unsaved man to accept Jesus.

Week 5, Day 3
This Unit: Our Ministry
Today: Handling Excuses 2

Read Luke 14:16-24

A TRUE STORY . . .

Jim was 29 years old. He said to a witnessing Christian, "I will never become a Christian because I will never believe there is a hell!"

How would you respond?

_____

_____

_____

DID YOU ANSWER JIM'S EXCUSE, OR DID YOU PROBE?

Many believers will seek to "reason" with him about the reality of hell. To do so is to fall into the Great Debate! No—probing is needed. Why did he make that statement? Of all the comments possible, why has he chosen the problem of hell? There's more to this than the surface objection explains!

MORE ABOUT JIM . . .

He loved and respected his father, who had died one year earlier. As far back as Jim could remember, his dad had searched through the writings of world religions, looking for

truth. Prior to his death, his father had told his son he had rejected all religion. He died without any form of faith.

Aha! The *probe method* uncovered the deeper issue: if Jim adopts a Christian belief, he feels he will eternally doom his own father—a man he loves deeply, still in grief over his death. By rejecting Christianity, he seemingly "spares" his father an eternal separation from God.

What can be done to reach him? Perhaps a comment like this would be appropriate:

"Jim, I know you have a strong distaste for hell. Do you know that God despises it even more than you or I do? Let's think again about John 3:16. It says that whoever believes in His son *shall not perish, but have ever-lasting life*! Is that not what you desire for yourself—everlasting life?"

OUR METHOD IS LOVE, LOVE, LOVE!

The beginning of our message is, "God so LOVED the world..." Don't just talk about His love—be His love! Display that love in dealing with excuses. It will be more powerful than any answer you may say with your lips.

How does that love manifest itself? God gave us the special chapter about it in I Corinthians 13. Meditate on it. To live this way is not only difficult for humans: it is impossible! That is why Paul reminded us that it is CHRIST who lives in us. In Him, this love can flow. Apart from him, it cannot.

SOME COMMON EXCUSES

1. "I HAVE ALWAYS BEEN A CHRISTIAN."

   Probe for the source of this excuse: "According to your understanding, what must one do to become a Christian?" (Review John 1:12-13)

2. "RELIGION WAS CRAMMED DOWN MY THROAT AS A CHILD. I WANT NOTHING MORE TO DO WITH IT!"

   Probe for the source of this excuse: "I sense you resent your parents for forcing you to go to church activities?" (Listen to answer.) "How do you feel about God? Is it only your parents you resent, or do you resent Him as well?" (Be prayerful about the way you proceed . . .)

3. "I DON'T REALLY FEEL A NEED TO DO THIS."

   Probe for the source of this excuse: "Have you had contact in the past with religious groups who emphasized that you have to have a *feeling* before you can become a Christian?" (Review John 1:12-13, pointing out that the focus is on *receiving*, not *feeling*. If there is no change in the person's spirit, be hesitant to pursue the discussion.)

4. "I NEED TO STUDY THE BIBLE MORE."

   Probe for the source of this excuse: "I would consider it an honor to share a brief Bible study with you, using a special booklet prepared for those wanting to know more."

5. "THERE ARE SO MANY HYPOCRITES IN THE CHURCH. I DON'T WANT TO BECOME LIKE THEM."

   Probe for the source of this excuse: "I sense you have some real hurts about people who go to church and who are not all they claim to be. Can you share with me the one that is most significant to you?"

   Listen sensitively to the answer. It may be a deeply emotional experience for the person to verbalize this hurt. If the excuse has truly been caused by hypocritical conduct, you may wish to say,

   "I hurt with you about this. Let me show you how Jesus felt about hypocrites: let's read Matthew 23:13-15: (Read it together.) Do you feel our Lord Jesus has the power to enable you and me to follow Him without becoming a hypocrite?"

Review these five commonly heard Excuses until you have mastered the responses to them. Jot down words you feel might be more appropriate to use:

_____

_____

_____

_____

_____

_____

WEEK 5, DAY 4
THIS UNIT: OUR MINISTRY
TODAY: ANSWERING SINCERE QUESTIONS

Read John 3:1-16

As you share the John 3:16 presentation, certain questions may be asked. Unlike excuses, these questions are sincere probes about areas of the Christian message of concern to the seeker. In most cases, they must be dealt with before a decision can be made. Often, the person has asked these questions before and has not received a satisfactory answer.

Be sure to use the *Probe Method* with questions. You will be far more effective in responding if you understand *why this problem is important to this person.*

Of all the dozens of possible problems, what has caused *this* one to become significant? For example, a person asks, "Do you think all people who die without Christ will go to hell forever?" Before quickly responding, it's important to have some background!

What is the previous experience which is triggering this question? Perhaps this person is thinking about a mother or father who died without personal faith. To accept this teaching, your friend would eternally condemn that parent.

Logically, we know what we *believe* does not change *truth,* but people do not always think rationally. Therefore, it is important to know what the impact of your answer will be.

WHAT ANSWERS ARE THOROUGHLY BIBLICAL?

A superficial answer should be avoided! Use scripture for everything you say. If you cannot do so, simply say: "I am not prepared to give you the answer you need. Let me do some digging, and I'll talk with you about that very soon."

As you review the most commonly asked questions in this lesson, underline each scripture verse. In the side margin, write a brief description of the question the verses answer. Using a page in the front or back of your Bible, list these excuses and all the verses you have underlined. Then, when a question is asked, you will be ready to use your Bible!

HAVE YOU SATISFACTORILY ANSWERED THE QUESTION?

If your answer leaves the person with a furrowed brow or questioning eyes, your response has been inadequate. Probe again! If you need to seek further aid, do so. Become a true servant to your friend.

OFTEN ASKED QUESTIONS

WHY DOES GOD PERMIT SUFFERING?
- GENESIS 3:1-24: The cause of suffering is man's sin and rebellion.
- ROMANS 8:19-22: Man's rebellion causes suffering everywhere. The whole earth groans because of it.
- ROMANS 8:18: As long as man rebels against God, suffering will continue.
- 2 CORINTHIANS 1:3-7: God does not send us suffering; He gives us comfort.

HOW CAN A MAN OF SCIENCE BELIEVE IN MIRACLES?

- GENESIS 1:1, JOHN 1:1: God created all matter in the first place.
- JOHN 1:3: The God who created all matter in the first place certainly has the power to suspend any natural law at any time.
- JOHN 2:11, 23; 4:54: Miracles always have a definite spiritual purpose. They reveal His presence and power.
- Science is a yardstick used to measure natural laws. It is totally incapable of measuring anything else. For example, science cannot measure love, hate, evil, or goodness. Such realities are not measurable by scientific procedures. It is also incapable of measuring the suspension of natural laws. Thus, a man of science must accept the limitations of his field.

HOW CAN GOD CONDEMN THOSE WHO HAVE NEVER HEARD ABOUT CHRIST?

- ROMANS 1:18-32: Men are condemned because they have rejected God's revelation of Himself through the creation. This revelation is universal. All men everywhere have equally received it.
- ROMANS 10:9-15: Men are not lost by not hearing of Christ. They are lost because they rejected His revelation through creation. Men are saved by hearing of Christ. But, hearing of Christ means absolutely nothing to men who have rejected God's revelation through creation. Millions of Americans have heard of Christ, and are lost!
- PSALM 8: No person is condemned because he has not heard the Gospel. Because that person has rejected the full revelation of God, brought through creation, they are condemned. What God has created is a "picture book," which can be "read" by the most illiterate heathen or the most educated Ph.D.

- HEBREWS 11:6: God is obligated to reveal Christ and His salvation to any person who truly seeks Him. In Acts, we see Him responding to Cornelius and the Ethiopian Eunuch by sending Peter and Philip to them.

CAN I LIVE THE CHRISTIAN LIFE?

- COLOSSIANS 1:21: A logical question for an unbeliever to ask! For a lifetime, this person has been "in charge" of life, and is programmed to carry out all decisions made. This decision will change all that! It is a decision to let Christ take charge.
- HEBREWS 4:10: There is a "rest" which is immediately given to the new Christian. It is up to the Christ who comes to live in us to live the Christian life.
- JOHN 14:15: The greatest joy of becoming a Christian is discovering the activity of the new King, making the decisions. Further, the relationship with Him is one of love, not obligation.
- JOHN 14:16: When I become His servant, He gives me a resource I never possessed before.
- JOHN 16:13, 2 CORINTHIANS 5:17: When, as a servant, I disobey, the Holy Spirit immediately "notifies" me, and He also makes the strong pull of my old desires disappear.
- 1 JOHN 1:9: Each time I find myself returning to the old pattern of self-rule, I need only "confess" (agree with God) that this is not what is proper, and His rule is again established.

 Return to these pages as you encounter these questions. Be sure to mark these verses in your Bible and keep a list of the scriptures for each question.

Week 5, Day 5
This Unit: Our Ministry
Today: Review John 3:16 Diagram

Read Acts 28:31

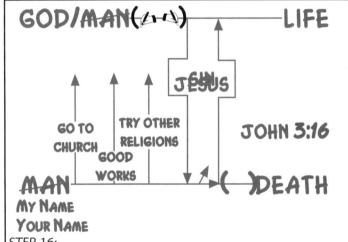

GOD/MAN(   )   LIFE

SIN
JESUS

GO TO   TRY OTHER
CHURCH   RELIGIONS   JOHN 3:16
               GOOD
               WORKS
MAN   )DEATH
My Name
Your Name

STEP 16:
But consider what it has already cost you! All these years you have lived without God's guidance. You have missed His perfect will for your life up to now. You will never know what your life might have been like if you had come to God years ago. That's why it's important for you to make this choice right now!

When drawing these two brackets, tenderly ask, "What regrets would you not have right now about your past if you had made the decision to let Christ direct your life three years ago, or five years ago, or ten years ago? We all have past memories which would be different if we had only come to Christ earlier in our life."

Think about your own past. Prayerfully consider what you would like to openly share about how Christ's guidance would have made a difference in your past. Even since you have become a Christian, are there experiences you regret when you failed to let Him rule over you as He should have? You will need these thoughts when talking to "Type A" unbelievers. Take a moment right now to write below areas you would like to share:

_____

_____

_____

_____

_____

_____

_____

_____

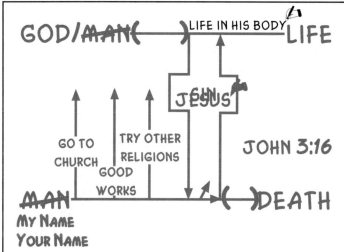

GOD/MAN(⟩LIFE IN HIS BODY LIFE

JESUS

GO TO CHURCH

TRY OTHER RELIGIONS

GOOD WORKS

JOHN 3:16

MAN

⟩DEATH

MY NAME
YOUR NAME

STEP 17:

When you come to the cross, Jesus sets you free from the penalty of sin. But there is much more! He enters your body, mind, and emotions. Then he immediately attaches you to others who have also asked Jesus to reign over them. I am a part of one of these groups that make up Christ's body. I want you to join it also, so we can continue to be guided by Christ in His body, which we call a "Cell Group."

Satan's greatest deception is to let a person accept Christ without any understanding that the body of Jesus Christ is a vital part of our salvation from the *power* of sin. Perhaps you are one of those Christians who for years thought of your relationship with Christ as *separate* from His body.

The concept of "church" as an add-on, an option to the Christian life, is not scriptural and will surely destroy the new believer. Think about this: *if the problem all along has been rebellion against Christ's ownership, then the Christian life must include His total control of our activities.*

The first official act of the Holy Spirit is to baptize us into the Body of Jesus. This means being attached to the "basic Christian community," the cell group, where we can edify one another. If this is not explained clearly to the unbeliever, you will have produced another Christian who detaches life in His body from being a Christian.

We have already considered this point in great detail in your Daily Growth Guides for Week Two. It is now time for you to think through how you will share this profound truth in presenting the plan of salvation.

Jot down what you will say in the space below:

_____

_____

_____

_____

_____

_____

_____

SHARING WITH YOUR CELL GROUP

During the weeks you will be contacting "Type A" unbelievers with your partner, your cell group should be informed about your ministry. On the following pages, there are worksheets you may use to prepare yourself for the *Share the Vision* times.

You do not have to use them in the order they appear. Select the one that seems "right" for you to share each week. It is anticipated that over the five weeks of this study, these would be the areas you would want to discuss with your group. Of course, you can change the topics if you prefer.

WHY YOU SHOULD SHARE WITH YOUR CELL GROUP

You and your partner should see yourselves as an extension of your cell group, not independent from it. You are ministering under their prayer intercession. They will have a keen interest in your activities.

Share with them the issues you are facing within your own life as a person, within your relationship as a team to each other, and with the "Type A" unbelievers you are touching. Help them know about the *oikos* contacts you are making through your contact with the unbelievers.

From time to time, you may wish to include someone from your Cell who would have a special affinity with someone you are ministering to.

OF COURSE, CONFIDENTIALITY IS IMPORTANT

Sometimes you will see there is a fine line between sharing needs in the lives of unbelievers for the purpose of intercessory prayer, and sharing information that should be kept confidential. If you have doubts about an area to share with the group, it is probably best not to talk about it. However, you may have one or two special people, including your cell leader or intern, with whom you can share the more personal issues.

REMEMBER THE IMPACT YOU WILL HAVE ON THE CELL

The "little children" in the Cell will profit greatly by learning about your journey into ministry. It will become a powerful model for them to copy in the days ahead.

Sharing About Your *Oikos* Contacts

NAMES WE WOULD LIKE TO SHARE:

_____

_____

_____

_____

_____

SPECIAL CIRCUMSTANCES OR STRONGHOLDS:

_____

_____

_____

_____

_____

FAMILY MEMBERS WHO NEED OUR PRAYERS:

_____

_____

_____

_____

PERSONAL NEEDS I HAVE OR WE HAVE AS A TEAM:

_____

_____

_____

_____

Sharing About Your Prayer Burden

NAMES WE WOULD LIKE TO SHARE:

_____

_____

_____

_____

_____

SPECIAL CIRCUMSTANCES OR STRONGHOLDS:

_____

_____

_____

_____

_____

FAMILY MEMBERS WHO NEED OUR PRAYERS:

_____

_____

_____

_____

PERSONAL NEEDS I HAVE OR WE HAVE AS A TEAM:

_____

_____

_____

_____

Sharing About Your
Investigative Bible Study

NAMES OF THOSE I AM MEETING WITH:

_____

_____

_____

_____

SPECIAL CIRCUMSTANCES OR STRONGHOLDS:

_____

_____

_____

_____

NAMES OF THOSE I DESIRE TO MEET WITH:

_____

_____

_____

_____

PERSONAL NEEDS I HAVE OR WE HAVE AS A TEAM:

_____

_____

_____

_____

Sharing About
Unbeliever's Strongholds

NAMES WE WOULD LIKE TO SHARE:

_____

_____

_____

_____

STRONGHOLDS NEEDING WARFARE PRAYER:

_____

_____

_____

_____

SITUATIONS RELATED TO STRONGHOLDS:

_____

_____

_____

_____

PERSONAL NEEDS I HAVE OR WE HAVE AS A TEAM:

_____

_____

_____

_____

Sharing About Your Cultivation Event

DATE/ DESCRIPTION OF THE EVENT WE ARE PLANNING:

_____

_____

_____

_____

_____

SPECIAL CIRCUMSTANCES NEEDING YOUR PRAYERS:

_____

_____

_____

_____

_____

NAMES OF THOSE WE WILL BE INVITING:

_____

_____

_____

_____

PERSONAL NEEDS I HAVE OR WE HAVE AS A TEAM:

_____

_____

_____

_____

REPORT FORM

(Duplicate five copies. The Team should present one copy each week for the five weeks of this training to the cell leader before the weekly meeting begins.)

Names of Team Members:

_____

_____

"Type A" Persons Contacted This Week:

_____

_____

_____

The John 3:16 Diagram was shared with the following:

_____

_____

_____

_____

Prayer requests we would like to include during *Share the Vision Time* in our meeting:

_____

_____

_____

_____

☐ We have met together for our Team meeting.

☐ We have both completed the Daily Growth Guides for Week ___

☐ We plan to have a get-together with "Type A" people on (date) ___/___/___

COMMENTS:

_____

_____

Signed:

_____

_____

REMOVE PAGE WITH SCISSORS ALONG THIS LINE

And without faith it is impossible to please God, because anyone who comes to him must believe that he exists and that he rewards those who earnestly seek him.

Therefore, my dear friends, as you have always obeyed—not only in my presence, but now much more in my absence—continue to work out your salvation with fear and trembling, for it is God who works in you to will and to act according to his good purpose.

Just as man is destined to die once, and after that to face judgment, so Christ was sacrificed once to take away the sins of many people; and he will appear a second time, not to bear sin, but to bring salvation to those who are waiting for him.

"For God knows that when you eat of it your eyes will be opened, and you will be like God, knowing good and evil."

For God so loved the world that he gave his one and only Son, that whoever believes in him shall not perish but have eternal life.

Hebrews 11:6

The prayer for one who says
"I am not ready,"

"Would you pray these words
and tell God you are seeking Him?"

Philippians 2:12-13

The way we find freedom from
the *power* of sin is through
Christ ministering to us through
one another.

Hebrews 9:27-28

Refers to salvation from the
penalty of sin and also
salvation from the *presence*
of sin.

John 3:16

The Gospel in a Nutshell

Genesis 3:5

The words of Satan to Eve;
the classic definition of the
source of all sin: *"be like God!"*